Color FOR THE WITHDRAWN Terrified Quilter

PLAIN TALK, SIMPLE LESSONS, 11 PROJECTS

Ionne McCauley and Sharon Pederson

Martingale ®
& COMPANY

Color for the Terrified Quilter:
Plain Talk, Simple Lessons, 11 Projects
© 2007 by Ionne McCauley and Sharon Pederson

That Patchwork Place® is an imprint of
Martingale & Company®.

Martingale & Company
20205 144th Ave. NE
Woodinville, WA 98072-8478 USA
www.martingale-pub.com

Printed in China
12 11 10 09 08 07   8 7 6 5 4 3 2 1

Library of Congress Cataloging-in-Publication Data
Library of Congress Control Number: 2006026570

ISBN: 978-1-56477-722-5

Credits

CEO: Tom Wierzbicki
Publisher: Jane Hamada
Editorial Director: Mary V. Green
Managing Editor: Tina Cook
Developmental Editor: Karen Costello Soltys
Technical Editor: Ellen Pahl
Copy Editor: Melissa Bryan
Design Director: Stan Green
Illustrator: Laurel Strand
Cover and Text Designer: Shelly Garrison
Photographer: Brent Kane

Mission Statement
Dedicated to providing quality products
and service to inspire creativity.

Dedication

To my entire family with many thanks for all your support,
and especially to Brian and Vicki for endless encouragement
and input (and for meals, housecleaning, and barn chores!)

~Ionne

To Gail and Heather, my extraordinary daughters

~Sharon

Acknowledgments

From Ionne

Many thanks to my quilting group, the Out to Lunch Bunch, for helping me start my career in teaching color classes, especially Beth who suggested it many years ago. I want to acknowledge all my students from whom I have learned so very much! The questions you have all asked have made me figure out many different ways to describe the same thing. A special thank-you to Bev, Linda, and Carol; Robin; Janet; Mary, Cathy, Fran, and Marilyn; and especially Dianne—all of you have promoted my classes for years. I couldn't have done it without you! Most of all a huge thank-you to Sharon, for her unfailing help, patience, great soup, and keeping me moving along when the lambing got in the way. The team at Martingale earns my heartfelt thanks for making this process enjoyable and smooth.

From Sharon

Thanks to Sy for not complaining about the dining room table becoming a desk again, and for carrying Ionne's bed back and forth from the barn; to my friends, who get ignored whenever a deadline looms but who never abandon me; and, as always, to the incredible team of people at Martingale who help me recognize the difference between good ideas and bad ones and—bless them—publish the good ones.

From Both of Us

We would both like to thank our extraordinary technical editor, Ellen Pahl, for her wit, her patience, and her ability to find the best combination of words to say what we mean. A big thanks to Brent Kane, the perfect photographer for a book on color—he is a true color artist. And last but not least, to Judie Hansen—thanks for providing the incubator.

Thanks also to Hobbs Bonded Fibers for all their excellent products. We've both used Electric Quilt software for years and would like to thank the company for producing a great program. And we couldn't have done all of this without our trusty Bernina sewing machines!

CONTENTS

How does that line from *The King and I* go—from your students you'll be taught? That was certainly the case for me. I met Ionne McCauley when she took a class from me many years ago. Over the years we've become very good friends, and when I needed help getting all the quilts made for *More Reversible Quilts*, she was the one I turned to. We had so much fun doing it, we decided that we had to write a book together.

The idea for *Color for the Terrified Quilter* came to me at 4:00 a.m. one morning and by 8:00 a.m. I had a pretty good outline to show Ionne. Now, you have to understand that the tables have definitely been turned and I am very much the student in this situation. My color choices have always been more or less intuitive, and it has been a great pleasure working alongside Ionne on this project. I have learned so much, I feel confident in saying that after you've absorbed all she has to teach you, color will no longer be a problem for you.

~Sharon

I love teaching students of all levels about using color in their quilts. To watch them have "aha" moments is my favorite part of the job. I firmly believe anyone can learn—at his or her own pace—to make choices about colors that are satisfying and pleasing.

Remember when you learned to use a rotary cutter? Think back to when you discovered the importance of the ¼" seam allowance or mastered the rules of appliqué. You can also learn the guidelines (not rules) about putting colors together so they suit *you*.

So read through our book to get an overview of our approach and a feel for looking at color in this way. Choose a project and try the process. There's no need to jump in at the deep end—choose your favorite color first. Then with that successful project under your belt, you can progress with confidence through the rest of the color wheel.

~Ionne

Marketing has an enormous influence on how we use color. At the beginning of a season, the various trade associations representing the clothing and home-decoration industries issue the year's color forecasts—lime green, purple, rose red, or whatever. Because marketing is all about selling, the hope is that you will rush out and buy all new things to show how fashionable you are and therefore keep the economy moving ahead. Your emotions are exploited in the name of sales.

Interestingly, we all react differently to this kind of manipulation. One fun exercise is to get together with some quilting friends and ask them to bring one fabric in each of the following colors: sky blue, sunshine yellow, tomato red, forest green, teal, peach, and royal purple. We're sure you'll discover that your set doesn't match any of your friends'.

Each person's idea of those descriptive words is different. I mean, what kind of sky are you looking at? It could be an Arctic sky, a tropical sky, or a hazy, cloudy sky.

In the following photos, you can see what happens when students are set loose in Sharon's or Ionne's stashes with instructions to find fabrics that "match" those descriptive words.

Interpretations of sunshine yellow

Interpretations of tomato red

Interpretations of sky blue

Interpretations of forest green

Interpretations of teal

Interpretations of peach

Interpretations of royal purple

There are other emotional responses to color that influence your choices—some going way back to your childhood. Maybe your mom made you wear pink and you've hated it ever since. Cultural differences also affect the way you perceive colors. Actual physical differences in our eyes will cause us to see color differently as well.

So, our advice is that while you work through the exercises in this book and learn about color, forget about why you like or dislike a particular color. Ignore what advertising is telling you about which colors you *should* be wearing this year, and just work in your comfort zone—by choosing your favorite color. If you hate pink, we aren't going to make you use it…at first, but our guess is you'll enlarge your comfort zone as you gain experience.

One good reason to start with your favorite color is that you'll have lots of it and you'll be more experienced with it. As you progress through the book you'll be introducing some of your least favorite color families into your work, but by then you'll know how to manage them and we hope you'll come to the conclusion that every color has its place.

We've written this book for anyone who wants to know more about color. The simple exercises and easy-to-make quilt projects are designed to help you learn about color families and value. Doing the exercises and making the mock-up blocks before sewing allow you to learn about color before you commit your fabrics to the sewing machine.

Remember: when you do the exercises you are not making heirlooms, so there are no mistakes. Also, you can learn everything you have to know about each exercise on a small project. Even making only the mock-up sample blocks we've provided can teach you a lot. You will learn from everything you do with the mock-ups, even if it's that you don't like what you did. Make notes on the page as you work—if you don't like something, write down why you don't. Do your best to explain to someone (your best friend, your husband, the cat) *what* isn't working for you.

For practical reasons, the quilts in this book are small. However, all these quilts could be enlarged to queen-size projects if you wish. We both like to bring lots of samples when we teach, and airlines set weight limits. We can bring either two big quilts or many small quilts. Which would you rather see?

CHAPTER 1

COLOR 101

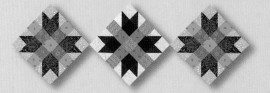

Learning about color theory may seem intimidating or send you scurrying away to do something else. But we've taken it upon ourselves with the writing of this book to simplify the process, making it easy and fun for even the most terrified among you. While we avoid most technical terminology, we do advocate the use of a color wheel. It is the standard tool of artists, designers, and many quilters when it comes to choosing colors. Just think of it as another highly useful notion in your sewing room. The diagram below is the standard 12-step color wheel. Each of the 12 colors is considered a "family."

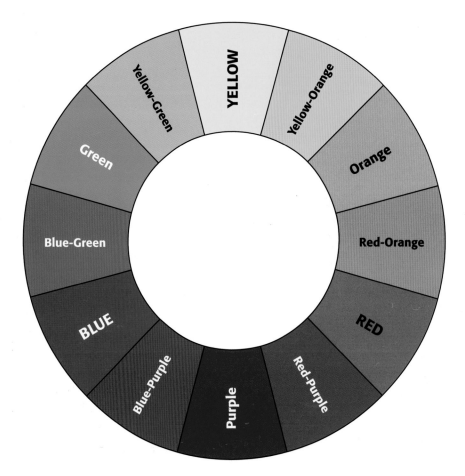

EXERCISE: Color Families

You will need to purchase a 12-step color wheel for this exercise, or use the one printed on page 8. Familiarize yourself with the names and relative positions of the color families. You may want to get together with a quilting buddy or two for this exercise.

Knowing that the color wheel we are using has 12 colors on it, think of each color as a family unit. Each color family consists of many family members—lights, mediums, darks, clear ones, and dull ones. Train yourself to think of the whole family instead of just one or two fabrics. Think of each piece of colored fabric as a member of that unit.

Now you will need your fabrics, leaving aside for the moment the multicolored ones. We will get to them later. Multicolored fabrics are those that represent more than one color family, such as the fabrics shown in the photo below.

Use primarily one-color fabrics for sorting.

Set aside multicolored fabrics.

When Ionne teaches this in class, she usually asks students to choose five or six colors and find as many different fabrics in each color as they can, making sure they have lights, mediums, and darks. The pieces can be medium-sized, but not larger than a fat quarter for classroom purposes. Students are told to be prepared to share once they get to class. There is no need to cut any fabric for this particular exercise. Fabrics will be used "as is" with no cutting; just fold them into manageable pieces. If you are at home, you can work with your entire stash if you like. The more you have to choose from, the better. At the end of the exercise, your fabrics will be neatly organized into color families.

Arrange all your fabrics into a circle like the color wheel. Start with your favorite color family. Yes, family! Let's choose blue as an example. Place all members of the blue family into a pile. Next to it place all the fabrics you can find that are blue-green, and then next to that, green and so on. You should be putting lights, mediums, and darks into the piles. You can even put in those that are a bit grayed or dusty looking—more about that later.

You may notice two things right away. One is that you will have gaps in your color families, and the other one is that your colors won't exactly match the color wheel. Don't worry about this— think of the wheel as a guide only.

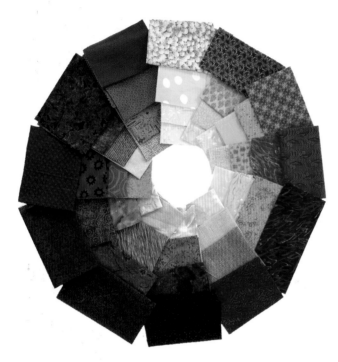

Arrange fabrics in a color wheel.

You will find that some fabrics seem to fall somewhere between two of the steps on the color wheel. For instance, you may have a blue-green fabric that is between blue-green and blue (a little more blue than blue-green). At this point you have to decide which family you want this fabric to belong to.

Trust your eye here. Use the color wheel to get started but try to resist matching the fabric to the paint chip at the edge of the wheel. Instead, think about the color of the fabric in relation to the colored fabric next to it. Take your time.

If you cannot figure out what color a particular fabric is, try the process of elimination. See where it doesn't fit on the color wheel, and then narrow it down some more until you find where it fits. The hard ones will be the grayed or muddy ones.

WHAT ABOUT BROWN?

We are often asked this question, "What about brown?" If you use the process of elimination, you will find that browns are usually grouped among the orange or red-orange families. Some browns may fit better in the yellow-orange group, and the occasional brown is a red-purple.

Some families will be better represented than others on your color wheel. We all have our favorites, and we tend to buy more fabric in that family than in others. For instance, if you are fond of the color green, many different variations will show up in your stash, from palest seafoam to darkest forest green. These are the green family members.

The green color family

From this exercise you have learned that there are many variations in the 12 color steps; in other words, there are many family members within each family unit. For example, moss green, avocado, and chartreuse are all just variations of yellow-green. Salmon, coral, peach, melon, and terra cotta are all members of the red-orange family. It can be confusing because we have so many different names for colors. No matter what the color is called, it will fit somewhere on the color wheel.

Now your sorted fabrics can be put into bins or on shelves according to color families.

Value

The most important thing to learn about color is value—what it is, and how to use it. Color is what attracts your eye, but value is what makes a pattern evident. Color is the star—value does the work. Value is the lightness, darkness, or even mediumness of a piece of fabric. Practice seeing beyond the color to evaluate the true value of a fabric.

Color may very well be the first thing about a quilt that catches your eye, but value changes are the characteristics that make the pattern or picture appear. So, in a sense, it doesn't matter what colors are in the quilt. If there are not enough changes in value or if the values are in the wrong places according to your design, the pattern won't work or will get lost. There are times when you may want the design or pattern to look lost, but you still need to know how to manipulate values to get the desired effect.

In this quilt, "Blue Plaid Shirt," we wanted to "lose" the Nine Patch pattern in the center of the quilt. See the photo of the complete quilt on page 30.

In this quilt the values are very distinct in the area with white background, resulting in a strong diagonal pattern in the Nine Patch blocks. See the photo of the complete quilt on page 80.

EXERCISE: Making a Value Scale

Within one color family are many values, everything from palest pale to darkest dark. A range of these values from lightest to darkest is called a value scale. Find six or seven fabrics ranging from light to dark in your favorite color family. Be sure to stay with immediate family members; just for this exercise, try to avoid going over to the neighboring color families. For instance, if you choose the green family, don't include any blue-greens or yellow-greens.

Arrange the fabrics from light to dark, left to right. Don't worry at this point if there are some that are grayed or muddy looking. All we need to worry about in this exercise is that all the fabrics belong to the same color family and are arranged from light to dark. If you take out the ones that don't "fit," soon you will notice more and more that don't fit, and you may end up with only two fabrics and you will have learned nothing. This exercise is only about value.

Fabrics arranged from light to dark

One fabric stands out because it is brighter,
but when you pull it out and lay it across the others,
you can see that it is medium.

When you have the fabrics arranged, cut 1" squares from each of them and arrange them, in the same order, on a sheet of white paper. Place them close together, overlapping slightly so that no paper shows between them.

Abrupt value changes will be very obvious if you look at them through the wrong end of binoculars or a reducing glass. Rearrange until you have the smoothest value flow you can manage.

Squares arranged from light to dark on paper

USE YOUR EYES

Practice seeing value relationships in everyday items such as signs, calendars, book covers, magazines, displays, produce aisles, and so on. This will hone your skills to perfection. Students often ask me about the red and green see-through value finders, but I encourage them to use their eyes, which they have with them at all times! After all, you don't look at quilts through value finders, do you? ~Ionne

You may have a few squares that are very similar. You'll know this if you can't decide where some of them go and you keep switching them back and forth. This usually means they are interchangeable as far as value is concerned. Another thing you might notice is that you will probably have more darks and mediums but not very many lights. This is extremely common; you are in good company. To correct this imbalance, you have our permission to go shopping!

Instead of discarding the duplicates, we suggest that you place them above and below where they fit. This makes the point that different fabrics can have the same value. A valuable lesson! (Pun intended!)

Double up squares of the same value.

Once your fabric swatches are arranged and you are happy with the value scale, use a glue stick and glue them in position. It's easier to apply the glue to the paper, and then place the fabric swatches on the glued area.

When a fabric has high contrast within the print, such as the ones shown in the next photo, we call it a "sparkle fabric." We mean by this that, when used sparingly, it behaves as an accent fabric. You can see one of these sparkle fabrics used in "Blue Plaid Shirt" in the photo on page 30. We use these fabrics to add sparkle or "jump" to our quilts. We feel that if all the fabrics in a quilt have the same density of print, the quilts end up with a flat appearance. There is not as much interest as when you use pieces of a sparkle fabric or busy print. However, the other extreme is to use too many of these kinds of prints together, at which point they cease to be accents. The decision to use this kind of fabric is very individual, so if you like this look, pursue it; if not, don't.

Sparkle fabrics

TRICKS TO CHECK VALUE

- Squint.
- Use a reducing glass or doorway peephole.
- Look through the wrong end of binoculars or through your camera lens.

EXERCISE: Relative Value

Value is relative, which means that fabrics behave differently depending on their surroundings or neighbors.

For this exercise, choose a color family to work with. You will need one light, two mediums, and one dark.

1. From the light, one of the mediums, and the dark fabric, cut two 1" x 3" strips. From the other medium, cut three 1" x 3" strips.

2. Arrange the light, medium, and dark strips on both sides of the "other" medium as shown.

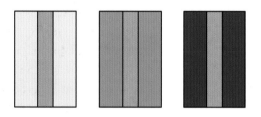

3. You can see that the same medium fabric behaves as a dark when surrounded by lights, as a medium when with other mediums, and as a light when among dark fabrics.

It's kind of like being the tallest kid in grade one, but when you hang out with grade two kids you're sort of in the middle, and if you wander into a high school class you are definitely going to be the short one. The following photograph illustrates this point with a green fabric. The same green appears as a dark, a medium, and a light, depending on the other greens. Understanding this effect can be used to your advantage.

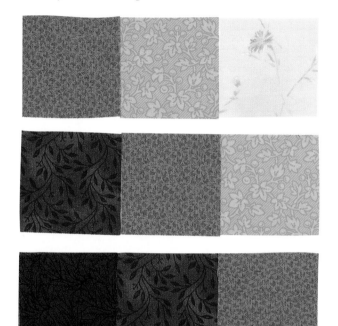

One medium green appears dark, medium, or light, depending on the neighboring fabrics.

Intensity

Color has intensity—meaning clearness or dullness. We call this the "in-your-face" factor. Is it in your face or, in other words, bright? If you answered yes, then it is intensely colored or clear. Is it dull or grayish looking? If yes, then it's a low intensity or murky family member—not less appealing, just less bright. This range of intensity can vary quite a bit. Some fabrics are only slightly dull and others are very dull, so much so that it's hard to even tell what color family they belong to!

You can have two fabrics from the same color family with the same value but different intensities. In other words they may both be light or dark but one will be clear and the other will be dull, or grayed.

Swatches on the left are grayed, duller versions of their partners on the right.

A black-and-white photocopy of a group of fabrics or a block can help distinguish between value differences and intensity differences.

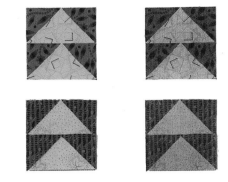

Value differences show up in black-and-white photocopies; intensities do not.

If there is only one grayed fabric in a quilt, it will wave and yell, "Look at me! Look at me!" If you give it some company (a fabric that's similar, but not necessarily the same), it will quiet down and have a conversation, making the whole quilt more interesting. Just as when we were arranging fabrics by value, if you always discard the one fabric that doesn't "fit," we can almost guarantee there will then be another one that doesn't fit, and this could go on to the point where there is nothing left. (Ask us how we know this!) A more positive approach, one that requires a bit more courage, is to add more of the same type into the quilt. Do you remember the song "I'm a lonely little petunia in an onion patch"? Well even if you don't, we think you can get the picture: one dull fabric mixed in with clearer ones is definitely going to be a lonely little petunia.

BRIGHT
WILL BE BRIGHT

If a fabric is in-your-face bright when you take it off the shelf in the shop, it will probably be in-your-face bright in the quilt as well. It's not going to change when you cut it up. This does not mean it's wrong to use the fabric; you just need to be aware of its character. The fabric may be one to consider using as an accent.

EXERCISES: Intensity

In the exercises that follow, you will learn to look for differences in intensity. Remember that intensity is not the same as value. Intensity has to do with how bright or dull the color is, and nothing to do with how light or dark it is. A few practice mock-up blocks will help you identify this aspect of color. You will also find out what happens when you move the intensely colored fabrics to different positions within a block. We chose to work with the green and blue families, but feel free to try a few different combinations with your favorites.

ABOUT MOCK-UPS

Mock-ups are a quick, easy way to try out color schemes and proportions of your chosen colors. You can also keep them for future reference and make notes in the margins about what you learned.

Throughout the book we have used six different blocks for mock-ups to try different color combinations. Gray-scale drawings of the blocks are shown on page 21. We find Girl's Favorite to be a very versatile block; it has many options for rearranging value differences to alter the look.

We have provided cutting instructions with the block diagrams for Sister's Choice and Girl's Favorite. The other blocks, Birds in the Air, Mrs. Taft's Choice, Mosaic No. 1, and Jewel Box, are all based on a 2" grid. Feel free to use other blocks of your choice as well.

When working with fabrics in your mock-ups and projects, remember to actually place the fabrics right next to each other to make decisions about them. It's impossible to guess what they will look like together until they are side by side.

Note: The cutting dimensions for the blocks are all finished sizes. That's another good thing about mock-ups—no seam allowances!

To Make a Block Mock-Up

1. Make at least two photocopies of the chosen block (pages 22 and 23), enlarging if desired.

2. Gather together a glue stick, pencil for making notes, rotary cutter, ruler and cutting mat, and maybe a cup of tea or coffee. We use an ordinary glue stick such as UHU. It does need to be a fresh one; sticky ones are impossible to use. And don't try to use rubber cement or a liquid glue.

3. Select fabrics and cut the patches for your chosen block using the dimensions provided with the block.

4. Using a photocopy of the block, called a mock-up sheet, arrange your fabrics on the block. Keep that glue stick capped for now. You may want to change a few fabrics around to get the effect you want. Be patient; sometimes you might go through several fabric choices for one area in the block before you make your final decision.

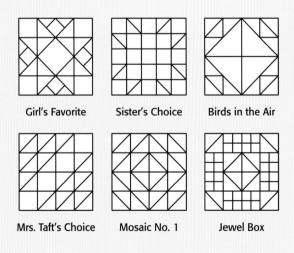

Girl's Favorite   Sister's Choice   Birds in the Air

Mrs. Taft's Choice   Mosaic No. 1   Jewel Box

EXERCISE 1: Intensity Mock-Up

You will make two mock-up blocks from each color family. Photocopy or trace the 5" Sister's Choice block on page 22 for these exercises.

1. From your stash, choose one light green for the C patches and two medium greens for the A and B patches. Their position in the two blocks will remain the same.

5. Once you're happy with the block, grab your glue stick. Here's a technical tip—put the glue on the paper, not the fabric. Apply glue to the second mock-up sheet, and then move your fabric pieces carefully and place them in position. Apply gentle pressure and smooth out the fabric to adhere it to the paper.

Save all your mock-up exercises for future reference. We highly recommend that you go back over your early mock-up sheets every now and then as you work through the exercises in the book. You will see how much you have learned; you'll discover that things fall into place and your choices become easier.

2. For D and E, choose two dark green fabrics of the same value but different intensities.

3. Make two block mock-ups, but switch the position of the two dark greens in the second block. Notice how the change in placement of intense colors can change the focus of the block. The only difference between the two blocks is the placement of the more intense dark green.

4. Now repeat this exercise with blue or another color family that is your favorite.

The focus of the blocks changes with the position of the more intense colors.

EXERCISE 2: Intensity Mock-Up

Green Blocks: Repeat exercise 1, but choose a dull green and a more intense clear green of the same medium value for the A patches. The other patches will remain the same in each block. Choose a light green for C, a dark green for B and E, and a medium green for D. See how this changes the look of the block.

Blue Blocks: Repeat exercise 1, but choose one medium for A, one dark for B and E, and one light for C. These will stay the same in each block. Choose two different fabrics for the D squares. One should be a grayed or less intense fabric and one should be a brighter or more intense version. A small change makes a major difference in the look of the block.

All fabrics are the same in both blocks except for the A patches.

We want to mention that just because we've shown you the dull one first and then the brighter one, this doesn't mean bright is better. Some of our favorite quilts and blocks have been in the less intense range.

Here is one more example of how dramatically different you can make a block look by a simple exchange of fabrics in one position. Which one do you prefer?

Warm and Cool

Here's one final thing to think about: The color wheel is basically divided into a warm side on the right and a cool side on the left. The cool side of the wheel consists of those colors that are associated with water, ice, and shadow or shade: yellow-green, green, blue-green, blue, blue-purple, and purple. The warm side consists of those colors related to fire, heat, and light: yellow, yellow-orange, orange, red-orange, red, and red-purple.

This is useful to know when you are trying to evoke a mood in a quilt. For instance, if you were attempting to convey a serene feeling you probably wouldn't use fire-engine red, but rather calming blues and greens.

Equally important is the fact that warm colors tend to advance, whereas cool colors appear to recede. If you want to emphasize one element of your design, choose a warm color for that area.

EXERCISE: Warm and Cool

For this exercise you will need one 6" x 6" square each of three warm colors (red, orange, and yellow-orange) and three cool colors (blue, green, and purple). From each square cut a 1"-wide strip and crosscut it into six 1" squares.

We've chosen not to pair up complementary colors (colors across the color wheel from each other) for this exercise. We want you to see the effect that warm colors can have when paired with cool colors, not necessarily their complement.

1. Begin with the red and blue fabrics. Referring to the photograph that follows, place the 1" squares loosely on their alternate rectangle.

2. Repeat step 1 with orange and green and then with yellow-orange and purple.

3. Put the pairs up on your design wall and stand back to take a look. Do you see that the warm red squares appear to be floating above the cool blue fabric? Likewise, when the red fabric is used for the background it tends to advance or come forward, while the blue squares look as if they are sinking into the red. Sometimes when we use a warm color as a background it comes so far forward that it takes over the design. Be careful with the placement of warm colors, especially if they are also intense warm colors. Some of these pairs will show a more subtle effect than others, depending on the color intensity—or lack of it—in your chosen fabrics.

Warm colors advance; cool colors recede.

Color 101 Review

Over the years, we've developed a mental checklist that we use when evaluating fabrics.

- Each piece of fabric has a color family to which it belongs.

- Each piece of fabric has a value, which is relative.

- Each piece of fabric has an intensity, which is also relative.

- Each piece of fabric belongs to either the warm side or the cool side of the color wheel.

Confusion arises because all these elements exist in every piece of fabric. By familiarizing yourself with these elements, you will be able to identify which characteristic needs attention if your color scheme isn't working.

No matter how many color families you incorporate into one project, you still need to group all the fabrics into lights, mediums, and darks, because value does the work of creating an effective appearance.

Three chosen color families

The three color families sorted into lights, mediums, and darks

Blocks for Mock-Up Exercises

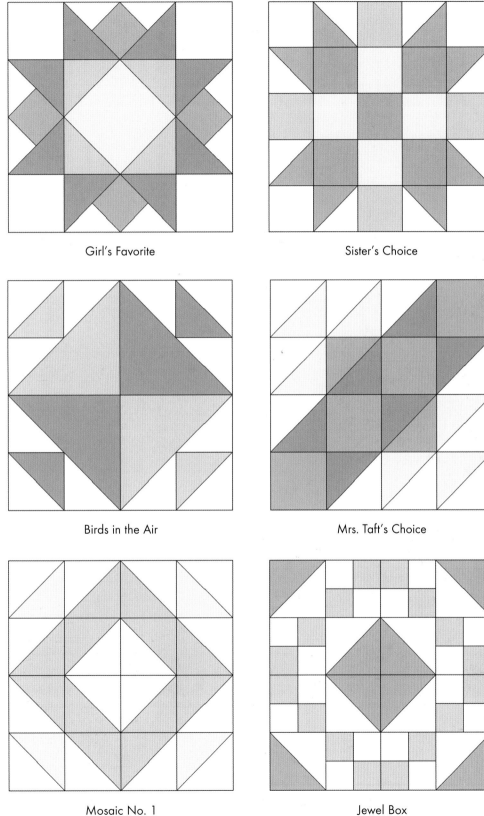

Girl's Favorite

Sister's Choice

Birds in the Air

Mrs. Taft's Choice

Mosaic No. 1

Jewel Box

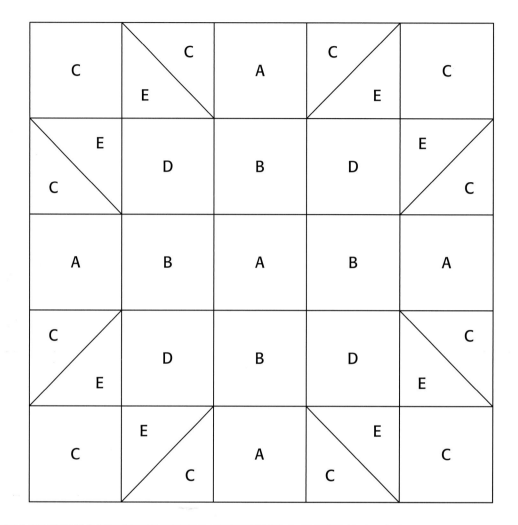

Cutting for Sister's Choice Mock-Up		
Pieces	Size to Cut for 5" Mock-Up	Size to Cut for 7½" Mock-Up*
A, B, D	1" x 1" square	1½" x 1½" square
C, E	1" x 1" square; cut once diagonally	1½" x 1½" square; cut once diagonally
*Enlarge the block diagram 150% for the 7½" block.		

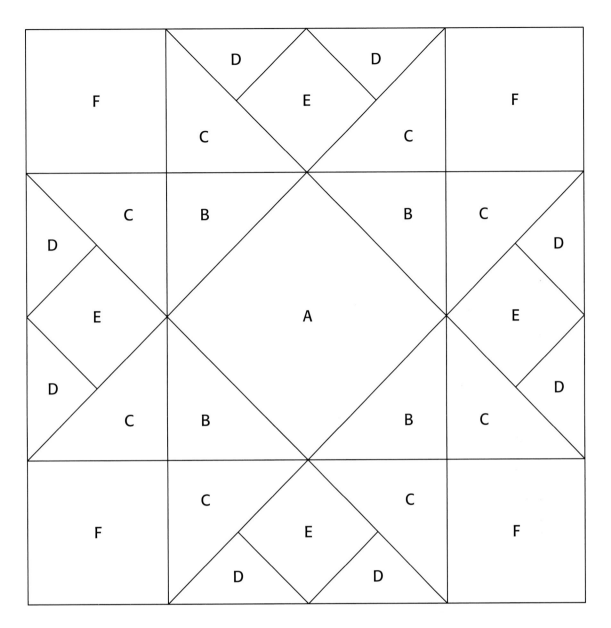

Cutting for Girl's Favorite Mock-Up		
Pieces	Size to Cut for 6" Mock-Up	Size to Cut for 8" Mock-Up*
A	2⅛" x 2⅛" square	2⅞" x 2⅞" square
B, C	1½" x 1½" square; cut once diagonally	2" x 2" square; cut once diagonally
D	1½" x 1½" square; cut twice diagonally	2" x 2" square, cut twice diagonally
E	1¹⁄₁₆" x 1¹⁄₁₆" square	1⅜" x 1⅜" square
F	1½" x 1½" square	2" x 2" square
*Enlarge the block diagram 133% for the 8" block.		

ONE COLOR FAMILY

ere's where we get acquainted with one color family, described by the technical term *monochromatic*. The important thing when working with just one color is to get the values—lights, mediums, and darks—to do the work for us. We like to use the term "job description" for values to make this easier to understand.

On page 26, you will meet the Greens. Think about green as coming from a large family that includes lights, mediums, darks, clear variations, and dull variations. As you choose fabrics from this color family, assign each one a job description—light, medium, or dark. You may want to have more than three classifications; feel free to include jobs for medium-light and medium-dark. You have to make these decisions for each fabric in every quilt—each one has a job to do, and you're the boss!

EXERCISE: Monochromatic Mock-Up

Because we both work with the software program Electric Quilt 5, our approach is usually to try things out on the computer first and then translate the ideas to fabric.

We experimented with some one-color-family mock-ups using the EQ5 version of Girl's Favorite, and we have shown two versions each of all 12 color families here. Notice how different the block can look depending on where you place your different values and intensities.

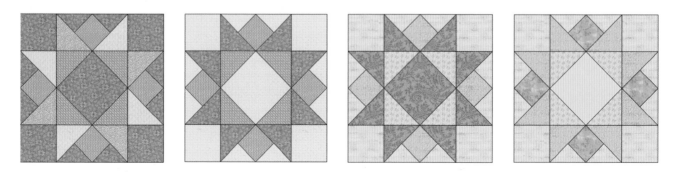

Girl's Favorite block mock-ups in monochromatic colors using Electric Quilt 5

Working with fabric is good, though, especially if you are just beginning to understand color concepts. On page 23 we've provided a 6" block known as Girl's Favorite for the exercises in this chapter. You can use the block in the size provided, but we suggest enlarging it to 8" because it's easier to get a feel for the fabrics. (Plus, you won't have to cut any $^1/_{16}$" measurements!) Refer to "About Mock-Ups" on page 16 for details on making a mock-up block.

1. Choose your favorite color; we've chosen green for some of the mock-ups and blue for others. Find as many fabrics in your chosen color family as you can: lights, mediums, darks, dulls, and brights. Sort them into value piles, because the value changes are what make the pattern.

2. Decide whether to have a light or dark background. For the first mock-up, you need to make an arbitrary decision. If light, choose two or three lights from your light-value pile. Then choose a medium and a dark—just to start. These are not final choices. For a dark background, choose one or two darks, then a medium and a light.

Block with dark background

3. Fold the fabrics into approximations of the shapes and audition them together until you narrow down your selection.

Block with light background

4. Once you have whittled down your selections, you can cut the patches for the block. Resist the urge to put the rest of your fabrics away, because if you do they will be "out of sight, out of mind" and you will forget what other choices you have available. Never tidy up unless the Queen is coming for tea!

For those of you who have a small stash, or those who suffer from "matchy-uppy-itis," refer to the following photographs to see what you can do with just one light, one medium, and one dark blue.

Blocks made with just three fabrics: one light, one medium, and one dark

However, think of what you could do with more than one light, one medium, and one dark. As a matter of fact, you can use two or three different lights, and only one dark or one medium—the proportions are up to you. You are making this, so you get to do what you like. It has to suit *you*. No one fails this class!

Block made of two lights, two mediums, and one dark

5. Referring to the block pattern for cutting dimensions, cut your fabrics. Using a photocopy of the block, called a mock-up sheet, cover each area with your chosen fabrics, but don't glue yet.

6. Refer to the color checklist that follows. We use this often; it's a methodical way of looking at your work when learning to define problem areas. Remember, this is a learning experience, not a high-speed information download!

COLOR CHECKLIST

- Is the value contrast where you want it?
- Are the lights, mediums, and darks in the right places?
- Can you see the shapes?
- Do some blend together? Is that what you want?
- Are the color families where you want them?
- Is there any one fabric that stands out too much because the intensity (clearness or dullness of color) is too different?
- Does it need more of the same kind of dullness or clearness?
- Check with a reducing glass, or squint to see the overall contrast of values.

7. When you're satisfied with the fabrics, apply glue to a second mock-up sheet, and then move your fabric pieces into position.

8. Step away from the block for a few minutes and then reevaluate it using the color checklist. Make notes in the margins about what you do and don't like, what you learned, the color family you used, value changes you want to try, and the date. This is the best place for these notes; you will refer to them many times, and if you date them it's fun to see how much your color choices improve over time.

Monochromatic - Blue Family
-not enough difference between dark and medium fabrics
- light fabric in the center stands out too much

-try a lighter medium and break up the light fabric

#1   10/25/51

Monochromatic - Blue Family
Better - more contrast between dark and medium, can see
      the "star" better
      -the light fabric broken up into 4 pieces is better

-I like the center "sparkle" fabric

#2   12/21/52

Make notes on your mock-ups and use them as reference.

When you're done, you may have some cut pieces of fabric left over. Save these for future exercises.

Make as many of these mock-up sheets as you like. Use a different color family; get together with quilting buddies and share fabrics. Move the positions of the darks, mediums, and lights to see how many options there are with just one block and different values of one color family. If something's not working, there's always "plan B."

Now that you are comfortable working with blocks in one color family, let's make a monochromatic quilt. The two quilt projects that follow are examples of monochromatic quilts.

SHARON AND IONNE'S TO-DO LIST

Here's our to-do list that we use for every quilt.

❑ Choose your color families.

❑ Separate all fabrics into lights, mediums, and darks.

❑ Assign a value, or job description, to each fabric.

❑ Do mock-up(s).

❑ Evaluate the mock-up using the color checklist on page 27.

We've included this list once within each of the following chapters to serve as a reminder.

BLUE PLAID SHIRT

few years ago I lost a younger brother to cancer. He very often wore an old, blue plaid work shirt. This quilt was not planned as a memorial, it just happened, which makes it even more special. I was putting together some previously cut strips to make a blue Nine Patch quilt for one of my color classes. My husband and I were talking about my brother while I was sewing the blocks into rows. As I turned to look at the last row of blocks, I realized with a jolt that I had made a quilt that looked like his blue plaid shirt. So, this one is for Raymond.

~Ionne

Materials

Yardage is based on 42"-wide fabric.

⅞ yard of medium blue tone-on-tone print for setting triangles

¾ yard *total* of assorted dark blue prints for Nine Patch blocks

⅜ yard *each* of two light blue tone-on-tone prints for setting squares

½ yard *total* of assorted medium blue prints for Nine Patch blocks

¼ yard *total* of assorted light blue prints for Nine Patch blocks

½ yard of fabric for binding

3 yards of fabric for backing*

44" x 50" piece of batting

If your fabric is 44" wide, 1⅝ yards will be enough.

Cutting

From the assorted light blue prints, cut:
54 squares, 2" x 2"

From the assorted medium blue prints, cut:
126 squares, 2" x 2"

From the assorted dark blue prints, cut:
198 squares, 2" x 2"

From the light blue tone-on-tone prints, cut:
30 squares total, 5" x 5"

From the medium blue tone-on-tone print, cut:
6 squares*, 9½" x 9½"; cut each square twice diagonally to yield 24 triangles (2 are extra)

2 squares*, 6" x 6"; cut each square once diagonally to yield 4 corner triangles

From the binding fabric, cut:
5 strips, 2½" x 42"

See the note on page 31.

29

Finished Quilt: 40" x 46" • Finished Block: 4½"
Made by Ionne

Note: By cutting the large squares into four triangles you maintain the straight grain on the edges so that you will not have a bias on the outside edge of your quilt. Similarly, by cutting the two smaller squares into two triangles the grain will also be on the outside when placed on the four corners. Make sure you keep the two sets of triangles separate, as they are similar in size.

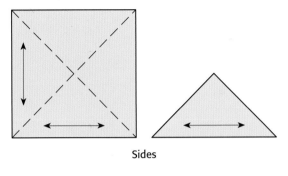

Sides

Corners

Making the Blocks

Referring to "Making a Scrappy Nine Patch" on page 84, construct 6 light, 14 medium, and 22 dark Nine Patch blocks, using the 2" squares. Press the seams to one side.

Make 6. Make 14. Make 22.

Quilt-Top Assembly

1. Arrange the Nine Patch blocks on your design wall on point, alternating them with the plain squares and referring to the quilt diagram and photograph for placement of the Nine Patch blocks.

2. Add the side setting triangles and corner triangles as shown in the diagram.

3. Sew the blocks and side triangles together in diagonal rows. Press seams toward the plain squares or side triangles.

4. Sew the rows together. Press all the seams in the same direction. Add the corner triangles last.

Finishing the Quilt

1. Referring to "Layering, Basting, and Quilting" on page 92, layer the batting, backing, and quilt top together. Baste with pins, or fuse if you're using fusible batting.

2. Quilt as desired.

3. Referring to "Binding" on page 94 , bind the edges of the quilt.

CHINESE COINS

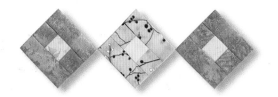

Thfs delightful little quilt is one we both want to keep. (I guess we'll have to make another one!) The block is based on a Nine Patch grid, but it looks like a square with a border.

We've made this elegant quilt in the yellow color family, but you can use your own favorite color. The fabrics we picked suggest an Asian theme, and the block centers evoke images of the holes in old Chinese coins. Fabrics printed with willow buds, various leaves, wood grain, and tropical fish lend themselves to this particular quilt. Try to find your own related group of prints. The very simple block makes value choices easy. Each block can be made with just two values—a light and a dark, or a light and a medium. We used a black-and-yellow print for the border.

~Ionne and Sharon

Materials

Yardage is based on 42"-wide fabric.

½ yard of black-and-yellow print for border

⅜ yard *total* of assorted dark yellow prints for blocks

⅜ yard *total* of assorted light yellow prints for blocks

⅜ yard of yellow print for binding

⅞ yard of fabric for backing

25" x 25" piece of batting

Cutting

From the assorted dark yellow prints, cut:
26 rectangles, 1½" x 3½" (13 matching pairs)

38 squares, 1½" x 1½" (13 pairs to match the rectangles; 12 for block centers)

From the assorted light yellow prints, cut:
24 rectangles, 1½" x 3½" (12 matching pairs)

37 squares, 1½" x 1½" (12 pairs to match the rectangles; 13 for block centers)

From the black-and-yellow print, cut:
4 pieces, 3½" x 25"

From the yellow print for binding, cut:
3 strips, 2½" x 42"

Finished Quilt: 21" x 21" • Finished Block: 3" x 3"
Made by Ionne

Making the Blocks

1. Using the 1½" squares cut from the yellow prints, make 13 units with light centers and 12 units with dark centers as shown. Press toward the darker print.

Make 13.   Make 12.

2. Add the 1½" x 3½" dark yellow and light yellow rectangles to the sides as shown to make 13 blocks with light centers and 12 blocks with dark centers.

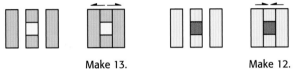

Make 13.   Make 12.

Quilt-Top Assembly

Refer to "Assembling the Quilt Top" on page 89 for tips on auditioning your blocks and sewing them together.

1. Referring to the quilt diagram, arrange the blocks in five rows of five blocks each, alternating the light and dark centers.

2. Sew the blocks together in rows. Press the seams in alternate directions from row to row.

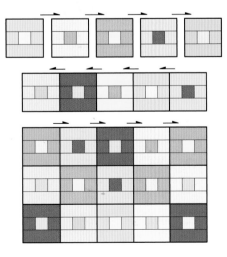

3. Referring to "Borders with Mitered Corners" on page 91, add the black-and-yellow print borders.

Finishing the Quilt

1. Referring to "Layering, Basting, and Quilting" on page 92, layer the batting, backing, and quilt top together. Baste with pins, or fuse if you're using fusible batting.

2. Quilt as desired.

3. Referring to "Binding" on page 94, bind the edges of the quilt.

SEAMS DIFFERENT

Working as a team has been an interesting experience, as we occasionally see things quite differently. Ionne made this quilt but Sharon drew the drafts of the illustrations. When we put the two together we realized that Ionne had sewn the blocks together quite differently from Sharon's drawing. Either way is fine and the quilt will look basically the same. However, the seams of the blocks alternate in Sharon's drawing, thus making construction easier because there are no seams to line up. Choose whichever method suits you.

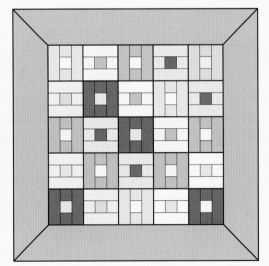

CHAPTER 3

THE NEXT-DOOR NEIGHBORS

You met the Greens in chapter 2 (the monochromatic gang). Now it's time to meet the next-door neighbors. These are the *analogous* colors. *Analogous* means related or similar. To work with analogous colors, choose color families that are side by side on the color wheel. You can have as few as two or as many as six, as long as they are next to each other. Always remember that value plays a major role, so you still need to have lights, mediums, and darks.

Using color families that are next-door neighbors can be a little more exciting than using just one color family. The effect is more enriched. Look around you for inspiration to come up with color families to use together. Look at a flower, for example. You'll often see more than one color family blended in the petals. In autumn you'll see related colors in the changing leaves and foliage—green, yellow-green, yellow, yellow-orange, orange, and even red-orange and red. You may want to limit yourself to three families to start off, but if you're feeling brave, venture into four or even five groups. And remember that you don't have to use equal proportions of the chosen color families. Consider using one of them as an accent. Refer to the color wheels below for the colors we used in the quilt projects.

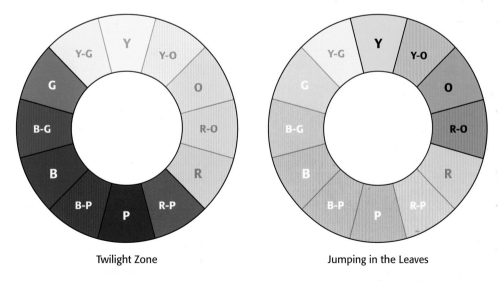

Twilight Zone   Jumping in the Leaves

Analogous colors

In this chapter you can have a lot of fun playing with next-door neighbor colors. You'll also be learning to distinguish family members and assign them jobs. Because value plays such an important part in our designs, it pays off to practice with different values before sailing forward into cutting and sewing. "Twilight Zone" has an over-under lattice effect that is easily accomplished but looks impressively complex! Careful observation of the three values used will give you practice at detecting slightly different values. Remember to stand back or use a reducing glass to check your value differences.

Because analogous color families have colors in common, it's easy to get a blended effect. These are great looks for landscape, sunset, and autumn colors. You will be using colors that are mixed from other colors. For example, if you mix red and yellow paint, you will get versions of red-orange, orange, and yellow-orange.

In "Jumping in the Leaves," we used an autumn palette of color families. Your choice of color families can really set a mood. Notice how the moods of the two quilt projects in this chapter are very different because of the color families chosen.

The color of the border fabrics can definitely alter the look of your project. For instance, because we used a medium blue for the border on "Twilight Zone," the quilt appears mostly blue. If you chose to use a purple border, the quilt would appear mostly purple.

FOLLOW THE DESIGNER

Fabric designers use color-wheel combinations to design and print multicolored fabrics such as those shown on page 9. We find these fabrics great for starting a quilt because all the colors are in one piece of fabric. Take a closer look at these and analyze which particular color scheme the designer used. You can find fabrics with the necessary colors already printed on them. These fabrics are sometimes known as bridging fabrics.

EXERCISE: Analogous Colors Mock-Up

For our examples we each chose a different mock-up block to work with. You may use any block that suits you for making mock-ups. In our opinion, the more different mock-ups you make, the more you learn.

The first block is Sister's Choice (page 22). We did two versions on Electric Quilt 5 and then chose one to do in fabric. You'll notice that the fabrics don't exactly "match" the EQ5 mock-up. It's good to keep in mind that exact matches are not always possible and that each exercise is worth doing in its own right, whether it's a mock-up on the computer or in fabric. You will learn from each one.

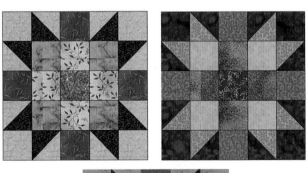

The second block is Birds in the Air (page 21). It is shown in six EQ5 versions, with three of them repeated in fabrics. Note that some of the same fabrics have been used in the two blocks using yellow-orange, orange, and red-orange. We changed the proportions of lights and darks and placed values in slightly different positions; this makes the blocks look quite different.

EQ5 Blocks

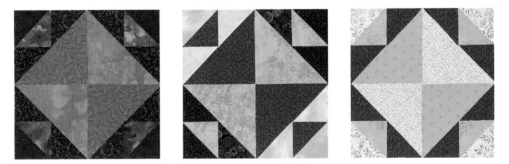

Fabric mock-up blocks

Refer to "About Mock-Ups" on page 16.

1. Select your analogous color families from the color wheel. Make a note of them on a sheet of paper. This makes it easier to keep track of which families you want to work with. As you choose your fabrics, remember to include a wide variety of lights, mediums, and darks in all your families.

2. Cut pieces to size according to the block you have chosen to use for this exercise. Remember that this is only a mock-up and that you are checking to see how color, value, and intensity are working together. You will also get an idea of the proportions of colors and values you want to use.

3. Try using one of your color families as an accent only. In "Twilight Zone," we used the red-purple fabrics as the warm accent, so it appears to be sprinkled over the surface of the quilt.

4. Make another block or two using the same fabrics. For something completely different, reverse the positions of the light and dark fabrics. Be patient; this takes a bit of time and is worth doing—you will learn lots about your colors.

5. Be perfectly honest with yourself about the values you are using. Is that dark fabric dark enough? Try another fabric; you can't imagine—literally—what two fabrics look like together until they are actually right next to one another. Don't guess; put them together.

6. Make notes on the page about what you do or don't like. These can be as simple as "This fabric too light" or "Don't like the brightness or high intensity of this fabric."

7. Use the color checklist on page 27 to evaluate your mock-up blocks.

Now that you are comfortable with the analogous colors, it's time to enter the twilight zone and jump in the leaves!

☑ Choose your color families.

☑ Separate all fabrics into lights, mediums, and darks.

☑ Assign a value, or job description, to each fabric.

☑ Do mock-ups.

☑ Evaluate the mock-ups using the Color Checklist on page 27.

TWILIGHT ZONE

I visited old friends in Australia recently with my sister. These friends were like family to me when I lived there for several years a long time ago. One evening we had a barbecue on the beach in the northern part of Queensland. We all stood on the beach with the tide whispering in at our feet, looking at the wonderful soft, clear sky. The stars were unfamiliar to my sister and me, but the Milky Way was there! The cool shadowy colors of that evening, with a bit of sunset sky thrown in for warmth (red-purple), inspired the color family choices for this quilt. The block, appropriately, is called Friendship Star—another Nine Patch variation.

~Ionne

Materials

Yardage is based on 42"-wide fabric.

1 yard *total* of assorted dark green, blue-green, blue, purple, blue-purple, and red-purple prints for blocks

½ yard *total* of assorted medium green, blue-green, blue, purple, blue-purple, and red-purple prints for blocks

½ yard *total* of assorted light green, blue-green, blue, purple, blue-purple, and red-purple prints for blocks

½ yard of medium blue print for border

⅜ yard of medium blue print for binding

1⅛ yards of fabric for backing

34" x 40" piece of batting

Cutting

From the assorted dark prints, cut
20 squares, 2½" x 2½"
80 squares, 3" x 3"

From the assorted light prints, cut:
40 squares, 3" x 3"

From the assorted medium prints, cut:
40 squares, 3" x 3"

From the medium blue print for border, cut:
4 strips, 3½" x 30½"

From the medium blue print for binding, cut:
4 strips, 2½" x 42"

Finished Quilt: 30" x 36" • Finished Block: 6" x 6"
Made by Ionne

Making the Blocks

1. Referring to "Half-Square Triangles" on page 86, make 80 half-square-triangle units with the 3" squares of dark and light fabrics. Make 80 with dark and medium fabrics. Press seams toward the darker fabric. Trim the units to 2½" x 2½".

Make 80.   Make 80.

2. Arrange four dark-and-light triangle units and four dark-and-medium triangle units from step 1 with a 2½" dark square as shown. Sew the units into rows and sew the rows together to make the Friendship Star block. Referring to "Pressing Matters" on page 85, press the seams open. Make 20.

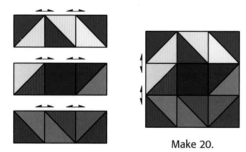

Make 20.

Quilt-Top Assembly

Refer to "Assembling the Quilt Top" on page 89 for tips on auditioning your blocks and sewing them together.

1. Sew the blocks together in rows, alternating the position of the blocks as shown in the diagram. Press the seams open.

2. Sew the rows together and press the seams open.

3. Referring to "Basic Borders" on page 90, sew the 3½" x 30½" medium blue strips to the sides of the quilt. Press seams toward the border.

4. Sew the 3½" x 30½" medium blue strips to the top and bottom of the quilt. Press seams toward the border.

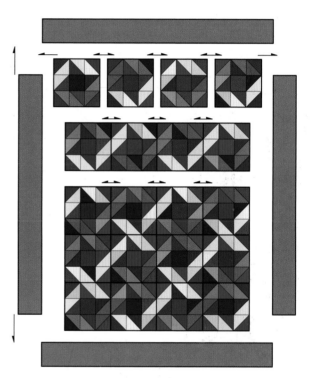

Finishing the Quilt

1. Referring to "Layering, Basting, and Quilting" on page 92, layer the batting, backing, and quilt top together. Baste with pins, or fuse if you're using fusible batting.

2. Quilt as desired.

3. Referring to "Binding" on page 94, bind the edges of the quilt.

JUMPING IN THE LEAVES

A ll those lovely leaves in the fall! When we were growing up, the raked piles were such fun to jump into. The smell of autumn is wonderful—spicy and smoky and cool at the same time. The next-door neighbor color families in this quilt are yellow, yellow-orange, orange, and red-orange. Remember that each of these warm colors, when darkened, can appear brownish. This means you could use light brown as well as peach if they suited your quilt, because they belong to the orange or red-orange families. Use lights and darks to create high-contrast blocks. If you want a softer effect with less contrast, use lights and mediums, or mediums and darks for a more mysterious evening effect.

~Sharon and Ionne

Materials

Yardage is based on 42"-wide fabric.

1½ yards *total* of assorted dark red-orange, dark orange (brown), orange, and dark yellow-orange prints for blocks

1 yard *total* of assorted light red-orange, orange, yellow-orange, and yellow prints for blocks

½ yard of fabric for binding

1⅝ yards of fabric for backing

40" x 52" piece of batting

Cutting

From the assorted dark prints, cut:
216 squares, 2½" x 2½"
36 squares, 3" x 3"

From the assorted light prints, cut:
144 squares, 2½" x 2½"
36 squares, 3" x 3"

From the binding fabric, cut:
5 strips, 2½" x 42"

JUMPING IN THE LEAVES

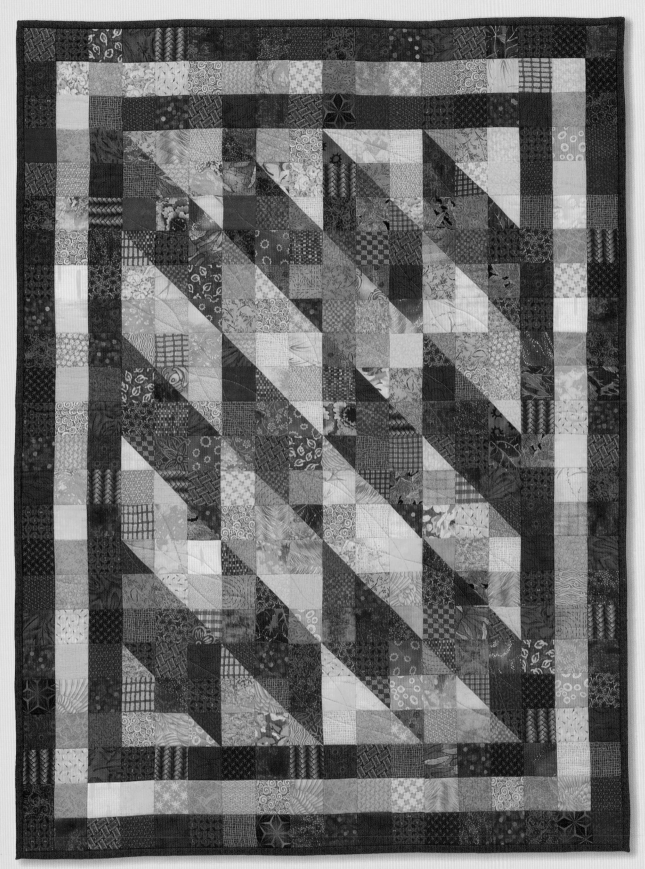

Finished Quilt: 36" x 48" • Finished Block: 6" x 6"
Made by Sharon

Making the Blocks

For the center of this quilt, you will make Split Nine Patch blocks. The blocks around the outside of the quilt are Nine Patches with a variation in color placement that allows them to act as a border. We find that this is often the easiest and nicest way to finish off a quilt. Besides, Sharon cut way too many squares for the blocks and she had to find a way to use them up!

1. Referring to "Half-Square Triangles" on page 86, use the 3" x 3" dark and light squares to make 72 half-square-triangle units. Trim them to 2½" x 2½".

2. Use the half-square-triangle units from step 1 and the 2½" light and dark squares to make a Split Nine Patch block as shown. Make 24 blocks.

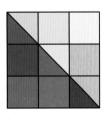

Make 24.

3. Use the remaining 2½" light and dark squares to make Nine Patch blocks as shown for the border.

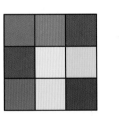

Make 4.   Make 20.

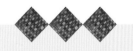

PRESSING ADVICE

This project is a good candidate for the "press seams open" version of the Nine Patch, which will make joining the blocks much easier. See "Pressing Matters" on page 85.

Quilt-Top Assembly

Refer to "Assembling the Quilt Top" on page 89 for tips on auditioning your blocks and sewing them together.

1. Referring to the quilt diagram, arrange the blocks on a design wall and sew them together in rows. Press the seams in alternate directions from row to row.

2. Sew the rows together and press the seams open or in one direction.

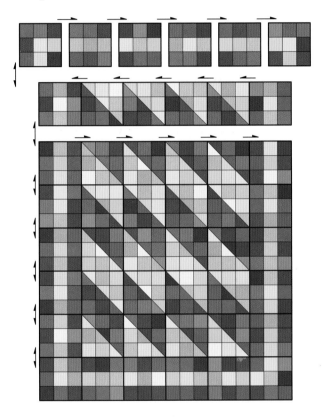

Finishing the Quilt

1. Referring to "Layering, Basting, and Quilting" on page 92, layer the batting, backing, and quilt top together. Baste with pins, or fuse if you're using fusible batting.

2. Quilt as desired.

3. Referring to "Binding" on page 94, bind the edges of the quilt.

THE FAMILY ACROSS THE ROAD

Now we'll introduce you to the family across the road, the complementary colors. Complementary color families are straight across the color wheel from each other. There are six possible combinations to work with and they always include one color from the warm side and one from the cool side of the wheel. Just because you are choosing two families to play with doesn't mean you have to use them in equal proportions, however. Feel free to use one family as the accent. Refer to the color wheels below for all the possible complementary color combinations and for the colors we used in the quilt projects.

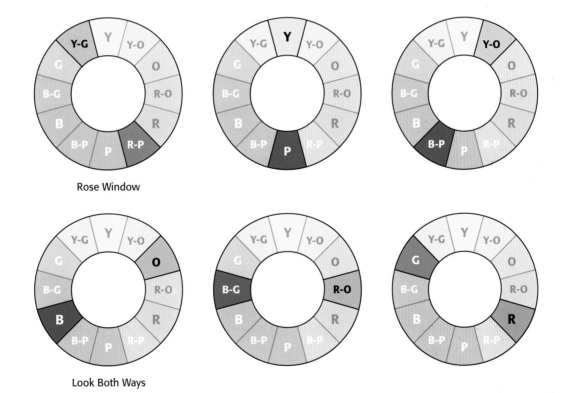

Rose Window

Look Both Ways

Complementary colors

In this chapter we've given you two different projects. "Rose Window" is a very bright, intensely colored quilt. If you like the color families in this project, but not the intense versions, you might decide to make your quilt in more muted fabrics. The other quilt, "Look Both Ways," is actually a very subdued version of the warmest (orange) and coolest (blue) color combination on the color wheel. If you like brighter blues and oranges, by all means use them instead. Just remember that value does the work; refer back to the sections in chapter 1 about value, intensity, and warm and cool colors for help if you need it.

Ionne says: Working with complementary color families has always been the most fun for me. I've found it exciting to work with these opposites. We show one blue-and-orange project in this chapter, but I feel like I have just touched on the possibilities using this combination.

When you're working with complements you have just two families to deal with, but because they are opposites, they will accentuate one another. This means that each fabric will appear brighter when placed next to its complement. You can test this by choosing, for instance, one red-orange fabric to use with all blue-green fabrics when you make a mock-up block. Then make another block using the same red-orange fabric in the same position and surrounding it with different versions (values) of red-orange or the neighboring color families of red and orange. You'll notice that the red-orange fabric sings much more loudly when it's among its complementary colors!

In the project "Rose Window," the strong versions of each color family sing loudly for two reasons: they are both intense versions and they are directly across the wheel from each other. This creates high drama.

"Look Both Ways" uses more subdued colors, so the overall feeling is quieter and less dramatic. However, because the color families are complementary, the fabrics still appear rich; they allow each other to show more brightly.

EXERCISE: Complementary Colors Mock-Up

Refer to "About Mock-Ups" on page 16 as needed for specifics of making a mock-up block.

For this example we have used a block called Mrs. Taft's Choice, from the alternate blocks shown on page 21. As usual, we started with the EQ5 versions—one using yellow and purple and one using red and green families.

When we went to fabric, we found a print with yellow and purple on it. At first, on the computer, we had the complementary print in the center of the block. But when we used fabrics, we felt that the print was better as a bridge between the yellow and purple, so we changed the position. We would not have known this had we not shuffled pieces around to see what would happen.

Please note that the look of computer-rendered mock-ups will depend also on the printer you are using. Refer to "About Mock-Ups" on page 16 as needed.

1. Choose your own complementary pair of color families to work with. Make a note of them. Remember that a wide range of lights, mediums, and darks will give you choices as you work. Keep them in view. Remember our rule: never tidy unless the Queen is coming.

2. You may want to investigate your stash to see if there is a fabric with the two chosen colors already on it. Designers often use complementary color families in print fabrics. For instance, maybe you've found a gorgeous batik fabric with a yellow-green mottled background and red-purple designs on it. You might make the entire quilt using many different yellow-green fabrics. If the red-purple color family is already represented, you don't have to look for any more red-purple fabric. This is a bit like using one of your two colors as an accent. Why not? Remember that you don't have to use equal amounts of the two color families in the quilt.

3. Change the positions of the fabrics; try a different dark or light. Each time you move fabrics around, you will have new possibilities, new proportions of colors to consider. If you don't try, you may never know how wonderful that particular fabric would have looked next to that other one!

4. Use the color checklist on page 27 to evaluate your mock-up blocks.

You're ready to move on to the quilts now. Complementary colors will be a fun walk in the park!

☑ Choose your color families.

☑ Separate all fabrics into lights, mediums, and darks.

☑ Assign a value, or job description, to each fabric.

☑ Do mock-ups.

☑ Evaluate the mock-ups using the Color Checklist on page 27.

ROSE WINDOW

hen my daughter was born, a friend gave me an unusual gift of two beautiful rose bushes. These bushes have survived the pruning efforts of my small flock of sheep and are now "sheep high," meaning they are basically woody stems up to where the sheep can't reach! Above that level, the roses bloom profusely each year. "Rose Window" brings to mind the hot pink roses of early summer and the fresh greens of the leaves. The glowing center of the quilt is like the sun streaming through the leaves. We've used the complementary colors of red-purple and yellow-green.

~Ionne

Materials

Yardage is based on 42"-wide fabric.

1 yard *total* of assorted medium yellow-green prints for blocks

⅞ yard *total* of assorted red-purple prints for blocks

⅝ yard of red-purple print for inner border and binding

½ yard of muddy yellow-green print for outer border

¼ yard *total* of assorted light yellow-green prints for blocks

⅛ yard of black print for blocks

2¾ yards of fabric for backing

46" x 46" piece of batting

Cutting

From the assorted medium yellow-green prints, cut:
128 squares, 2½" x 2½"
36 squares, 3" x 3"

From the assorted light yellow-green prints, cut:
12 squares, 2½" x 2½"
4 squares, 3" x 3"

From the assorted red-purple prints, cut:
96 squares, 2½" x 2½"
32 squares, 3" x 3"

From the black print, cut:
16 squares, 2½" x 2½"

From the red-purple print, cut:
2 strips, 1" x 36½"
2 strips, 1" x 37½"
5 strips, 2½" x 42"

From the muddy yellow-green print, cut:
2 strips, 2¾" x 37½"
3 strips, 2¾" x 40"

Finished Quilt: 41½" x 41½" • Finished Block: 6" x 6"
Made by Sharon

Making the Blocks

1. Referring to "Half-Square Triangles" on page 86 and using the 3" squares, make 8 half-square-triangle units with light yellow-green and medium yellow-green fabrics, and 64 units with red-purple and medium yellow-green fabrics. Trim them to 2½" x 2½".

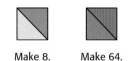

Make 8.   Make 64.

2. Using the 2½" squares and the half-square-triangle units from step 1, make 36 divided Nine Patch blocks as shown.

Make 12.   Make 4.   Make 20.

Quilt-Top Assembly

Refer to "Assembling the Quilt Top" on page 89 for tips on auditioning your blocks and sewing them together.

1. Arrange the blocks on a design wall, referring to the quilt diagram. Sew the blocks together in rows. Press the seams in alternate directions from row to row.

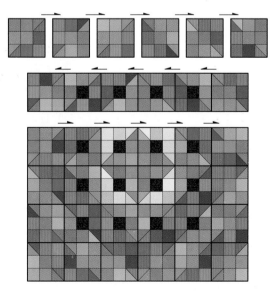

2. Sew the rows together and press the seams open or in one direction as desired.

3. Referring to "Basic Borders" on page 90, sew a 1" x 36½" red-purple piece to each side of the quilt. Press seams toward the border.

4. Sew a 1" x 37½" red-purple piece to the top and bottom of the quilt. Press seams toward the border.

5. Sew a 2¾" x 37½" muddy yellow-green piece to each side of the quilt. Press seams toward the red-purple border.

6. Sew the three remaining 2¾" x 40" muddy yellow-green pieces end to end. From this strip cut two pieces, 2¾" x 42", and sew them to the top and bottom of the quilt. Press seams toward the red-purple border.

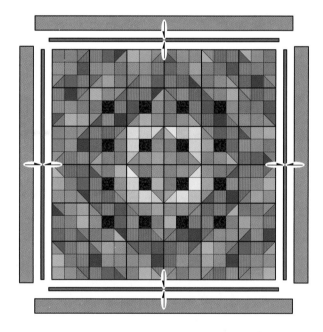

Finishing the Quilt

1. Referring to "Layering, Basting, and Quilting" on page 92, layer the batting, backing, and quilt top together. Baste with pins, or fuse if you're using fusible batting.

2. Quilt as desired.

3. Referring to "Binding" on page 94, bind the edges of the quilt.

LOOK BOTH WAYS

Do you remember your parents telling you to look both ways before crossing the street? I do, and along with that memory is an even sweeter one—the feeling of a strong hand holding mine while I crossed that dangerous-looking street. These are the same colors (and in some cases even the same fabrics) I used in the memorial quilt I made after my father died. While I was making this one he was very much on my mind, and looking at the quilt reminds me of all the happy times we had together.

The crossing paths on this simple Nine Patch variation look both ways from the center of the color wheel. We used a dull orange batik with a very grayed blue print. The combination of large and small Nine Patches continues the theme of a small child feeling the protection of a loving parent.

~Sharon

Materials

Yardage is based on 42"-wide fabric.

1 yard of gray-blue tone-on-tone print for blocks

⅔ yard of gray-blue print for outer border

½ yard of dull orange batik for blocks

⅓ yard total of assorted dull orange prints for blocks

¼ yard of dull orange print for inner border

½ yard of fabric for binding

2¾ yards of fabric for backing

47" x 47" piece of batting

Cutting

From the gray-blue tone-on-tone print, cut:
5 strips, 4¼" x 40"; cut into 41 squares, 4¼" x 4¼"

6 strips, 1¾" x 40"; cut into 48 squares, 1¾" x 1¾", and 32 rectangles, 1¾" x 3"

From the assorted dull orange prints, cut:
68 squares, 1¾" x 1¾"

From the dull orange batik, cut:
3 strips, 4¼" x 40"; cut into 20 squares, 4¼" x 4¼"

From the dull orange print for border, cut:
2 strips, 1¼" x 34¼"
2 strips, 1¼" x 35¾"

From the gray-blue print for border, cut:
2 strips, 4" x 35¾"
3 strips, 4" x 40"

From the binding fabric, cut:
5 strips, 2½" x 40"

Finished Quilt: 42¼" x 42¼" • Finished Blocks: 11¼" x 11¼"
Made by Sharon

Making the Blocks

1. Make four small Nine Patch blocks as shown, using five 1¾" dull orange squares and four 1¾" gray-blue squares. Press toward the gray-blue squares.

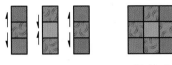

Make 4.

2. Using the dull orange 1" squares and the gray-blue 1¾" x 3" rectangles, make eight blocks and eight reversed blocks.

Make 8.   Make 8 reversed.

3. Using the small Nine Patch blocks made in step 1, the blocks from step 2, and the 4¼" gray-blue squares, make four Nine Patch blocks as shown.

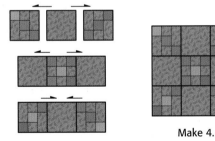

Make 4.

4. Using the 4¼" dull orange batik squares and the 4¼" gray-blue squares, make five Nine Patch blocks as shown.

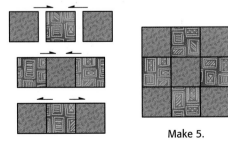

Make 5.

Quilt-Top Assembly

Refer to "Assembling the Quilt Top" on page 89 for tips on auditioning your blocks and sewing them together.

1. Arrange the blocks in three rows of three blocks each as shown in the quilt diagram.

2. Sew the blocks together into rows. Press the seams in alternate directions from row to row.

3. Sew the rows together and press the seams open or in the same direction as desired.

Adding the Borders

1. Referring to "Basic Borders" on page 90, sew the 1¼" x 34¼" dull orange border strips to the sides of the quilt. Press seams toward the border.

2. Sew the 1¼" x 35¾" dull orange border strips to the top and bottom of the quilt. Press seams toward the border.

3. Sew the 4" x 35¾" gray-blue border strips to the sides of the quilt. Press seams toward the dull orange border.

4. Join the three 4" x 40" gray-blue border strips together end to end and cut into two pieces, 4" x 42¾".

5. Sew the 4" x 42¾" gray-blue border strips to the top and bottom of the quilt. Press seams toward the dull orange border.

Finishing the Quilt

1. Referring to "Layering, Basting, and Quilting" on page 92, layer the batting, backing, and quilt top together. Baste with pins, or fuse if you're using fusible batting.

2. Quilt as desired.

3. Referring to "Binding" on page 94, bind the edges of the quilt.

CHAPTER 5

A FORK IN THE ROAD

While we're across the road, we'll meet the other neighbors, split-complementary families. A *split-complementary* group of families can be found using an isosceles triangle on a color wheel. (An isosceles triangle is one with two sides of equal length.) This gives you three color families to work with, always remembering that they can be used in unequal amounts. This color grouping has 12 possible combinations.

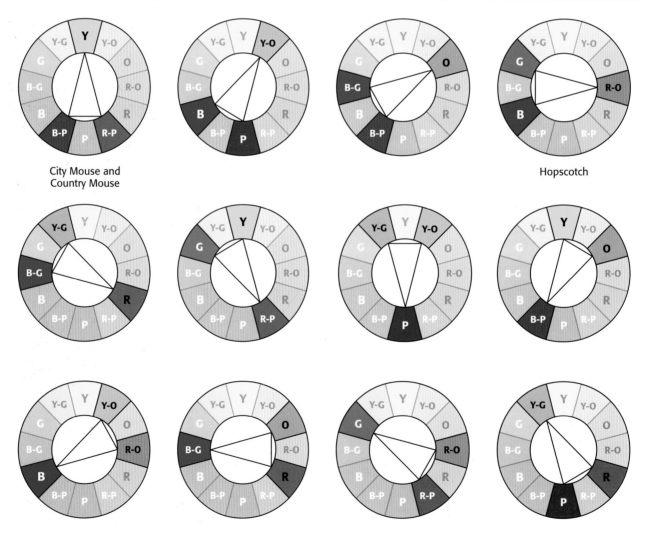

City Mouse and
Country Mouse

Hopscotch

Split-complementary colors

There are two quilt projects in this chapter: "Hopscotch" and "City Mouse." We've included a photo of a third quilt, "Country Mouse," which is simply a bright version of the color combinations of yellow, blue-purple, and red-purple. Note that in "Hopscotch" we used an extra color family, blue-green, which falls between the two at the base of the triangle. This is a good example of not letting the "rules" inhibit your choices. The red-orange is used sparingly, serving as an accent color. What is appealing about a quilt is often the proportion of color families used. The proportion of red-orange is small, but important. The proportion of colors to each other is an aspect of learning about color that is often overlooked.

Let's Talk about Yellow

The quilts "City Mouse" and "Country Mouse" both use yellow as one of the three colors. Many people find yellow hard to work with or shy away from it because they're not sure how to use it in a quilt. It's often hard to determine the value of a yellow.

A common mistake made by quilters is to classify bright yellow as dark. When asked to choose dark yellow, students frequently choose bright or intense yellows instead. Remember, *dark* is a value term, not an intensity term. If two yellows of the same value are used side by side in a block, the pattern may disappear.

In the examples above right, you can see what happens when bright is used in place of dark. In the yellow block in the top pair, the star points are brighter, but that is because the fabric is intense, strong, or vivid, not because it is dark. The dark star points in the yellow block on the bottom have more value contrast and are more easily visible from a distance.

Some other names that dark yellow is often called are gold, bronze, yellow-brown, and mustard. If you have trouble classifying a fabric in the yellow family, try the process of elimination. Where else on the color wheel can your gold or bronze fabric fit? You'll find that it doesn't fit anywhere but among its other yellow family members.

Bright star points on the top left have less contrast than dark star points (bottom). The bright star points fade in the black-and-white photocopy because they are the same value as the background.

When in doubt about value differences as opposed to intensity differences, photocopy the fabrics in question in black and white. Intensity differences don't show up in black and white, but value differences do, as shown in the photograph above.

On the left in the photograph below are two piles of yellow fabrics. These are both light yellows, but the top group is much more intense than the lower group. The four fabrics on the right are darker yellows.

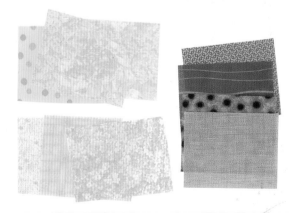

Intense light yellows and dull light yellows on the left, and dark yellows on the right

EXERCISE: Split-Complementary Colors Mock-Up

When you become more familiar with the many different members in each color family, you realize that you have an incredible range of choices. We have made some mock-ups using a very old traditional block called Mosaic No. 1. Here are two EQ5 versions and three fabric versions!

The first uses the color families of blue, yellow-orange, and red-orange. The red-orange was limited by "diluting" it, or choosing a very pale subdued value for the background area. It just adds warmth to the block and allows the almost complementary blue and yellow-orange to spark each other up.

The second samples of red, blue-green, and yellow-green were a surprise. We got so excited by the color combination we made on the computer that we just had to make that one too. Then we discovered in Sharon's stash a wonderful alternate dark yellow-green that would add movement to the background area. So we made that one too! Bet you can't make just one either!

Refer to "About Mock-Ups" on page 16 as needed for specifics on making a mock-up block.

1. Select three color families from the color wheel for your own version of a "Fork in the Road" block using Mosaic No. 1 on page 21. Refer back to the color wheels at the beginning of this chapter to choose one group. Remember that value does the work and that you are the boss!

2. As before, it is sometimes helpful to use one of your color families as the accent. Think about using the accent in two ways—the single representative from one color family and the clearest or most intense one—a double duty assigned to one color family. This is what is happening with the red fabrics in the two samples above.

3. Use the color checklist on page 27 to evaluate your mock-up blocks.

This chapter has the largest number of combinations to play with, so you will have lots of opportunities for exploring this neighborhood. Split complementary color combinations are lovely and rich. They are slightly less severe than direct complements can sometimes be.

Here's a hint: Check out your multicolored fabrics. Make a note of all the color families represented on them. You just might have one with your chosen group already on them—a great starting point!

Once you've mastered a few split-complementary mock-up blocks, you're ready to move on to make the quilts.

HOPSCOTCH

When I was going to grade school in Vancouver, British Columbia, we girls played hopscotch during recess and lunchtime. A big part of the game was choosing your marker. It seems that hopscotch players in Vancouver had a very unusual way of marking their spots—we used beads. In spring when hopscotch season was about to start, we would head to the five-and-dime to buy packages of seed beads. We spent hours stringing them onto thread in glorious color combinations. As well as marking our place in the game, they gave us hours of pleasure as we strung, chatted, and had show-and-tell. Of course there were many opportunities to bargain and trade for a coveted bead. I've talked to hundreds of women my age about what they used as markers when playing hopscotch, and so far I have not found any other area where beads were used.

~Sharon

Materials

Yardage is based on 42"-wide fabric.

1½ yards *total* of light, medium, and dark assorted blue, blue-green, green, and red-orange prints for blocks and outer border

⅞ yard *total* of assorted lights in blue, blue-green, and green for triangles

⅞ yard *total* of assorted darks in blue, blue-green, and green for triangles

⅔ yard of red-orange print for inner border and binding

3 yards of fabric for backing

50" x 50" piece of batting

Cutting

From the blue, blue-green, and green prints, cut:
268 squares, 2½" x 2½"

From the red-orange prints, cut:
17 squares, 2½" x 2½"

From the dark triangle fabric, cut:
18 squares 5⅛" x 5⅛"; cut each square once diagonally to yield 36 triangles

From the light triangle fabric, cut:
8 squares, 5⅛" x 5⅛"; cut each square once diagonally to yield 16 triangles

10 squares, 7¼" x 7¼"; cut each square twice diagonally to yield 40 triangles

Continued on page 59

Finished Quilt: 46" x 46" • Finished Block: 6" x 6"
Made by Sharon

Continued from page 57

From the red-orange print, cut:
2 strips, 1½" x 36½"
2 strips, 1½" x 38½"
5 strips, 2½" x 40"

Making the Blocks

1. Arrange the 2½" blue, blue-green, green, and red-orange squares into pleasing combinations. Referring to "Making a Scrappy Nine Patch" on page 84, make 13 Nine Patches.

Make 13.

2. Find the center of the long side of one dark triangle cut from the 5⅛" squares and match it to the center of a Nine Patch. Sew the triangle to the Nine Patch. Press the seam toward the triangle. Repeat for all four sides. Make nine blocks using the dark triangles.

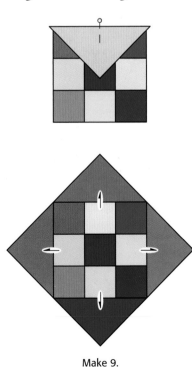

Make 9.

A PERFECT MATCH

If you fold the Nine Patch in half right sides together and finger-press, then fold the triangle wrong sides together and finger-press, the little creases that you created will fit together snugly when put together.

3. Repeat step 2 using the light triangles cut from the 5⅛" squares. Make four blocks.

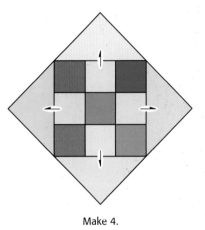

Make 4.

4. With the remaining light triangles (cut from the 7¼" squares), make four corner units and eight side units as shown. Be careful with the bias edges. Press.

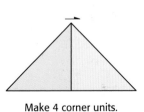

Make 4 corner units.

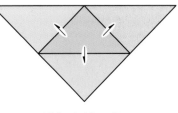

Make 4 side units.

Quilt-Top Assembly

1. Referring to the quilt diagram below, arrange the light and dark blocks, the side units, and the corner units in diagonal rows.

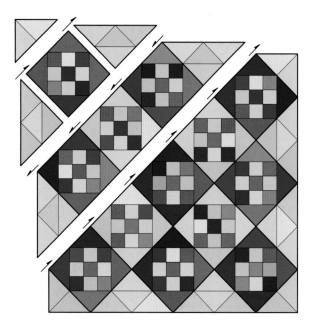

2. Sew the blocks and side triangles together into rows. Press the seams in alternate directions from row to row.

3. Sew the rows together, adding the corner triangle units last. Press the seams in one direction.

Adding the Borders

1. Referring to "Basic Borders" on page 90, sew a 1½" x 36½" red-orange piece to each side of the quilt. Press toward the border.

2. Sew a 1½" x 38½" red-orange piece to the top and bottom of the quilt. Press toward the border.

3. Piece the outer border with the remaining 2½" squares. The two side borders are made up of two rows of 19 squares each. The top and bottom borders are made up of two rows of 23 squares each. Place the red-orange squares randomly in the border, referring to the photograph on page 58 for approximate placement.

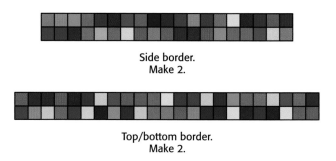

Side border.
Make 2.

Top/bottom border.
Make 2.

4. Sew the two side units to the sides of the quilt. Press toward the inner border.

5. Sew the two remaining units to the top and bottom of the quilt. Press toward the inner border.

Finishing the Quilt

1. Referring to "Layering, Basting, and Quilting" on page 92, layer the batting, backing, and quilt top together. Baste with pins, or fuse if you're using fusible batting.

2. Quilt as desired.

3. Referring to "Binding" on page 94, bind the edges of the quilt.

CITY MOUSE

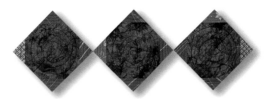

Interior-design magazines can be a great source of color combinations. We were discussing this one day and decided that we would do a "city" and a "country" version of the same quilt. A country look frequently uses bright colors, and a city look often uses a more sophisticated palette. The two quilts we made for this section use the same color combinations, but with those differences. "City Mouse" also has a mitered border, befitting this mouse's position as the sophisticated family member. Since it's unlikely that you will find a striped fabric wide enough (45") for mitered borders, we've written the instructions for cutting the fabric on the lengthwise grain so that the stripes run parallel to the quilt rather than at right angles. This gives you the same sophisticated look, but with the stripes going in a different direction.

~Sharon and Ionne

Materials

Yardage is based on 42"-wide fabric.

1⅜ yards of low-intensity (muddy) yellow striped fabric for outer border*

⅝ yard *total* of assorted low-intensity (muddy) yellow prints for blocks

⅝ yard of dark blue-purple print for blocks

½ yard of dark red-purple print for blocks

¼ yard of yellow print for inner border

½ yard of fabric for binding

1¾ yards of fabric for backing

44" x 44" piece of batting

*If you cut crosswise strips and piece them, ⅞ yard is enough.

Cutting

From the dark blue-purple print, cut:
26 squares, 2½" x 2½"
8 squares, 6½" x 6½"

From the dark red-purple print, cut:
22 squares, 2½" x 2½"
5 squares, 6½" x 6½"

From the assorted muddy yellow prints, cut:
112 squares, 2½" x 2½"

From the yellow print, cut:
2 strips, 1" x 30½"
2 strips, 1" x 31½"

From the muddy yellow striped fabric, cut:
4 strips, 5¼" x 45", on the lengthwise grain

From the binding fabric, cut:
5 strips, 2½" x 40"

Finished Quilt: 40½" x 40½" • Finished Block: 6" x 6"
Made by Ionne

COUNTRY MOUSE
Finished Quilt: 37½" x 37½" • Finished Block: 6" x 6"
Made by Sharon

Making the Blocks

1. Referring to "Making a Scrappy Nine Patch" on page 84, make 12 Nine Patch blocks using the 2½" dark blue-purple, dark red-purple, and assorted muddy yellow print squares.

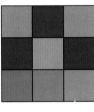

Make 12.

2. Referring to "The Snowball Block" on page 88, make 13 Snowball blocks using the 6½" dark blue-purple and dark red-purple print squares and the 2½" muddy yellow print squares.

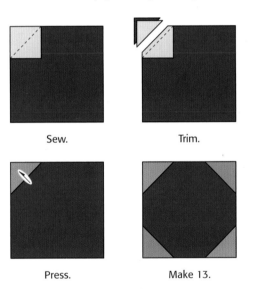

Sew. Trim.

Press. Make 13.

Quilt-Top Assembly

Refer to "Assembling the Quilt Top" on page 89 for tips on auditioning your blocks and sewing them together.

1. Arrange the Nine Patch and Snowball blocks in five rows of five blocks each, alternating the blocks as shown in the quilt diagram. Sew the blocks into rows. Press the seams in alternate directions from row to row.

2. Sew the rows together. Press the seams in one direction.

Adding the Borders

1. Sew a 1" x 30½" yellow strip to the top and bottom of the quilt. Press toward the border.

2. Sew a 1" x 31½" yellow strip to the sides of the quilt. Press toward the border.

3. Referring to "Borders with Mitered Corners" on page 91, sew the 5¼" x 45" strips of muddy yellow stripe to all four sides of the quilt.

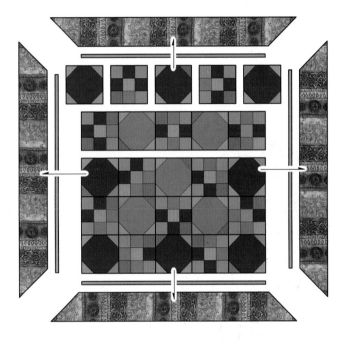

Finishing the Quilt

1. Referring to "Layering, Basting, and Quilting" on page 92, layer the batting, backing, and quilt top together. Baste with pins, or fuse if you're using fusible batting.

2. Quilt as desired.

3. Referring to "Binding" on page 94, bind the edges of the quilt.

CHAPTER 6

THE TRIPLETS

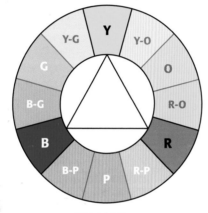he triplets make up the triad family groups. These are found on the color wheel by using an equilateral triangle, which is a triangle with all three sides of equal length. There are four possible combinations of triplet, or three-color, families.

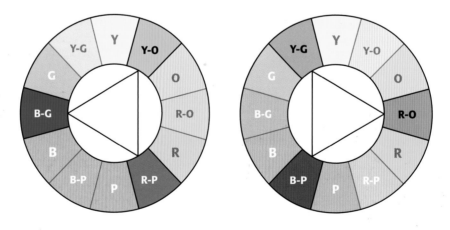

Midnight Stars

Copper Beech

Triad colors

Remember, multicolored fabrics are the ones with more than one color family represented, sometimes referred to as bridging fabrics. Even if they have only two parts of a three-family grouping, they are still useful for these color schemes. We've used bridging fabrics in both of the quilts in this chapter.

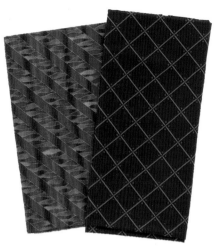

Multicolored fabrics can be used as bridging fabrics.

Color schemes such as complementary, split complementary, and triad (triplet) are starting points. You may want to add other colors to your mix. Notice that one of the pair has green added to the red-blue-yellow triad combination. Don't feel you must be a slave to the scheme.

When making the quilts in this chapter, feel free to choose your favorite color combination. Get all the family members out on your workspace. Refer to the sections in chapter 1 for help in choosing the versions of the colors that suit you.

EXERCISE: Triad Colors Mock-Up

For this chapter we've chosen to use another traditional block known to us as Jewel Box. See page 21 for a drawing. We first created a block using EQ5 and then made a similar mock-up in fabric.

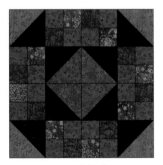

EQ5 block

Fabric mock-up block

Both blocks include the color families of red-orange, blue-purple, and yellow-green. You will notice again that in the computer-generated one the yellow-green fabrics are a bit darker than those in our fabric version. Try to resist matching fabrics to pictures. Find your own pleasing combinations. Computer-generated mock-ups can be used as a starting point.

Next, we chose to work with yellow-orange, red-purple, and blue-green. We also chose clearer and lighter colors. It's hard to believe these samples were made using the same block. This is another good example of how value placement can change the look of your pattern.

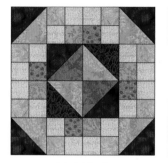 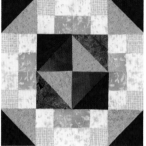

EQ5 block   Fabric mock-up block

There are only four possible combinations to work with in this chapter, so try playing a bit more with intensity differences and value changes.

Refer to "About Mock-Ups" on page 16 as needed for specifics on making a mock-up block.

1. Choose your triplet colors from the color wheels. Put all your fabric choices out in front of you.

2. Try the multicolored fabrics in your stash. Make notes about the color families represented on them.

3. Use the color checklist on page 27 to evaluate your mock-up blocks.

Carry on to make the quilts once you understand the triplet color concept and have a few mock-up blocks under your belt.

✓ Choose your color families.

✓ Separate all fabrics into lights, mediums, and darks.

✓ Assign a value, or job description, to each fabric.

✓ Do mock-ups.

✓ Evaluate the mock-ups using the Color Checklist on page 27.

COPPER BEECH

A lovely beech tree stands in the yard of our good friends Judie and Dick Hansen. The light flickers through the leaves and glints off the bark. A dark spruce tree crowds in close. In fall, our favorite time of year, we love the combination of coppery leaves and dark green branches. Purple shadows lie beneath the trees. These colors inspired us to look over the color wheel and we found that this is actually a time-honored combination of colors. There's no need to have equal proportions of the three color families either. The shaded area under the trees is quite small. We made this quilt with only four fabrics plus the purple accent color—quite a change from our usual multiple-fabric quilts.

~Sharon and Ionne

Materials

Yardage is based on 42"-wide fabric.

1 yard of medium orange print for blocks

1 yard of orange-and-green print for blocks and outer borders

1 yard of medium green print for blocks

½ yard of dark green print for blocks

⅓ yard of purple print for inner border

½ yard of fabric for binding

2¾ yards of fabric for backing

49" x 49" piece of batting

Cutting

From the dark green print, cut:
5 strips, 2½" x 40"; set aside 2 strips and crosscut 3 strips into:
    1 strip, 2½" x 14"
    36 squares, 2½" x 2½"

From the medium green print, cut:
2 strips, 2½" x 40"

1 strip, 2½" x 14"

2 strips, 10" x 40"; crosscut into 4 rectangles, 10" x 13", and 1 rectangle, 7" x 10"

From the medium orange print, cut:
2 strips, 2½" x 40"

1 strip, 2½" x 14"

2 strips, 10" x 40"; crosscut into 4 rectangles, 10" x 13", and 1 rectangle, 7" x 10"

Continued on page 69

Finished Quilt: 45" x 45" • Finished Block: 6" x 6"
Made by Ionne and Sharon

Continued from page 67

From the orange-and-green print, cut:
5 strips, 2½" x 40"; set aside 2 strips and crosscut
   3 strips into:
   1 strip, 2½" x 14"
   36 squares, 2½" x 2½"

2 strips, 3½" x 39½"

3 strips, 3½" x 40"

From the purple print, cut:
2 strips, 2" x 36½"

2 strips, 2" x 39½"

From the binding fabric, cut:
5 strips, 2½" x 40"

Making the Blocks

1. Sew the 2½" x 40" and 2½" x 14" dark green strips to the 2½" x 40" and 2½" x 14" medium green strips to make one short and two long strip sets. Press the seams toward the dark green fabric. Crosscut into 36 units, 2½" wide.

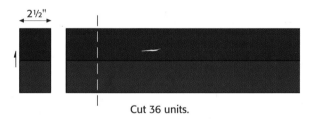

2½"

Cut 36 units.

2. Repeat step 1 with medium orange and orange-and-green print strips. Press toward the orange-and-green print.

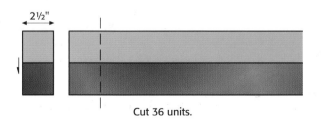

2½"

Cut 36 units.

3. Referring to "Mass Producing Half-Square Triangles" on page 87, draw a grid of twelve 3" squares on the wrong side of the 10" x 13" medium orange rectangles. Draw a grid of six 3" squares on the wrong side of the 7" x 10" medium orange rectangle. Make 108 half-square triangles using the medium orange and medium green fabrics. Trim them to 2½" x 2½". Refer to "Pressing Matters" on page 85 to choose which way the seams will be pressed.

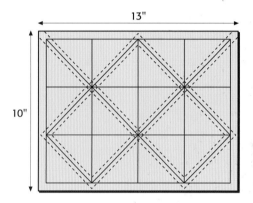

13"

10"

Make 4.

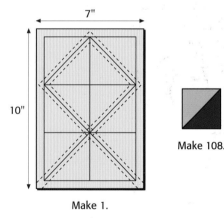

7"

10"

Make 1.

Make 108.

4. Referring to the diagram, use the units made in steps 1 and 2, the half-square triangles made in step 3, and the 2½" dark green and orange-and-green squares to make 36 Nine Patch blocks.

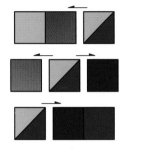 

Make 36.

Quilt-Top Assembly

Refer to "Assembling the Quilt Top" on page 89 for tips on auditioning your blocks and sewing them together.

1. Arrange the blocks in six rows of six blocks each, rotating every other block 90° as shown in the quilt diagram.

2. Sew the blocks together in rows. Press the seams in alternate directions from row to row.

3. Sew the rows together. Press the seams in one direction.

Adding the Borders

1. Referring to "Basic Borders" on page 90, sew the 2" x 36½" purple strips to the top and bottom of the quilt. Press toward the purple border.

2. Sew the 2" x 39½" purple strips to the sides of the quilt. Press toward the border.

3. Sew the 3½" x 39½" orange-and-green print border strips to the quilt sides. Press toward the orange-and-green borders.

4. Join the three 3½" x 40" border strips end to end. Cut into two strips, 3½" x 45½", and sew to the top and bottom of the quilt.

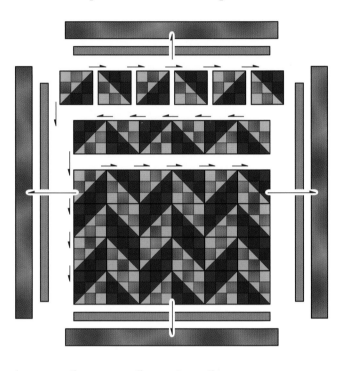

Finishing the Quilt

1. Referring to "Layering, Basting, and Quilting" on page 92, layer the batting, backing, and quilt top together. Baste with pins, or fuse if you're using fusible batting.

2. Quilt as desired.

3. Referring to "Binding" on page 94, bind the edges of the quilt.

MIDNIGHT STARS

When we began designing quilts for this book, we thought we would keep things simple. We didn't want to make anything too complicated when the point of the book is to become more confident about your color choices. However, we both decided that it is a short jump from half-square triangles to quarter-square triangles, and we couldn't resist throwing them in. The Ohio Star block is one of our favorites. We both live in the country, far from the bright lights of a town, so our night sky (when it isn't raining) is spectacular. You don't have to get very far from the lights of the house to be into some serious darkness. We've tried to capture this in "Midnight Stars."

~*Ionne and Sharon*

Materials

Yardage is based on 42"-wide fabric.

⅞ yard of dark blue geometric print for outer border

⅞ yard of medium blue print for Snowball blocks, corners of light blue Snowball blocks, and Ohio Star blocks

½ yard of medium light blue print for Ohio Star blocks

⅜ yard of red print 1 for blocks

⅓ yard of dark blue print for corners of medium blue Snowball blocks

¼ yard of red print 2 for inner border

¼ yard of light blue print for the four light Snowball blocks

⅛ yard of yellow print for the center of the 5 Ohio Star blocks in the quilt center

⅛ yard of dark yellow (gold) print for the center of outer Ohio Star blocks

½ yard of fabric for binding

2⅔ yards of fabric for backing

48" x 48" piece of batting

Finished Quilt: 44" x 44" • Finished Block: 6" x 6"
Made by Sharon and Ionne

Cutting

From red print 1, cut:
3 strips, 3¼" x 40"; crosscut into 34 squares, 3¼" x 3¼"

From the medium light blue print, cut:
2 strips, 2½" x 40"; crosscut into 32 squares, 2½" x 2½"

2 strips, 3¼" x 40"; crosscut into 24 squares, 3¼" x 3¼"

From the medium blue print, cut:
8 squares, 6½" x 6½"

1 strip, 3¼" x 40"; crosscut into 10 squares, 3¼" x 3¼"

4 strips, 2½" x 40"; crosscut into 52 squares, 2½" x 2½"

From the yellow print, cut:
5 squares, 2½" x 2½"

From the dark yellow (gold) print, cut:
12 squares, 2½" x 2½"

From the light blue print, cut:
4 squares, 6½" x 6½"

From red print 2, cut:
4 strips, 1½" x 40"

From the dark blue print, cut:
2 strips, 2½" x 40"; crosscut into 32 squares, 2½" x 2½"

From the dark blue geometric print for border, cut:
4 strips, 6½" x 32½"

From the binding fabric, cut:
5 strips, 2½" x 40"

While deciding about color families and values for "Midnight Stars," we made a few EQ5 mock-ups using the Girl's Favorite block on page 23. Most of this was done to decide on the right yellow fabrics for the different areas of the quilt. We decided to go directly to fabric because the yellows in EQ5 were not what we wanted.

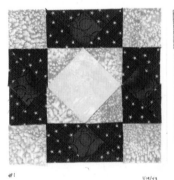

Shown are the four fabric mock-ups with different fabrics and notes explaining how we arrived at the final color choices. Even though we used a different block in the quilt, you can see how this process can be helpful.

Making the Blocks

1. Referring to "Quarter-Square Triangles" on page 88, make the following units using the 3¼" squares of red print 1, medium light blue print, and medium blue print.

Make 28.   Make 40.

2. Using the quarter-square triangle units from step 1 and the 2½" squares of medium light blue print, medium blue print, yellow print, and gold print, make the Ohio Star blocks as shown below. Set aside the four blocks for the borders.

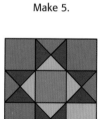

Make 5.

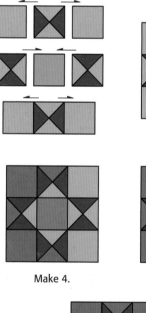

Make 4.   Make 4.

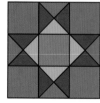

Make 4.

3. Referring to "The Snowball Block" on page 88, make four blocks with 6½" light blue squares and 2½" medium blue corner squares. Make eight Snowball blocks with 6½" medium blue squares and 2½" dark blue corner squares.

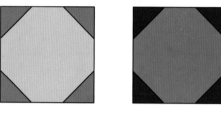

Make 4.   Make 8.

Quilt-Top Assembly

Refer to "Assembling the Quilt Top" on page 89 for tips on auditioning your blocks and sewing them together.

1. Referring to the quilt diagram, lay out the Ohio Star and Snowball blocks in five rows of five blocks each as shown.

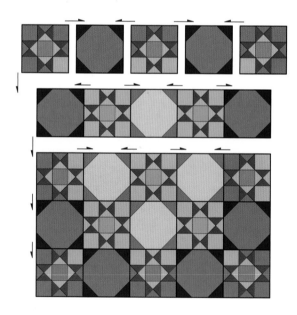

2. Sew the blocks together in rows and press the seams toward the Snowball blocks.

3. Sew the rows together; press the seams in one direction.

Adding the Borders

1. Referring to "Basic Borders" on page 90, measure your quilt and sew a 1½" red print 2 border strip to the sides of the quilt.

2. Sew a 1½" red print 2 border strip to the top and bottom of the quilt.

3. Referring to "Borders with Corner Squares" on page 91, measure and cut four border pieces from the 6½"-wide dark blue geometric print strips. Sew a border strip to the sides of the quilt. Press the seams toward the red border.

4. Sew one of the remaining Ohio Star blocks to each end of the two remaining 6½" border strips.

5. Sew the pieced border strips to the top and bottom of the quilt. Press seams toward the red border.

Finishing the Quilt

1. Referring to "Layering, Basting, and Quilting" on page 92, layer the batting, backing, and quilt top together. Baste with pins, or fuse if you're using fusible batting.

2. Quilt as desired.

3. Referring to "Binding" on page 94, bind the edges of the quilt.

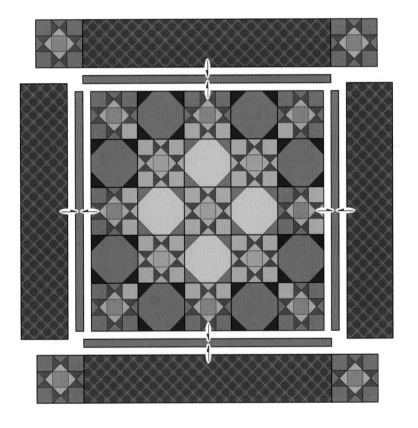

CHAPTER 7

THE FAMILY REUNION

When you put lots of colors together, the only way it will work is if you focus on value. This is where you can use all the leftover pieces from the quilts in this book. Once you begin combining all the color families, you're making scrap quilts. Go for it, kids! But remember—value, value, value!

Scrap or Multicolored Quilts

Scrap quilts are fun to make but can be troublesome without a knowledge of value. It's tricky to work with so many fabrics, but if you can choose color families and keep in mind that value changes are crucial in making the pattern evident, you are halfway there. The other troublesome aspect is intensity. We suggest that you reread "Intensity" on page 15 for review.

We can't tell you often enough that you must always think of the three aspects of every fabric you choose:

- It belongs to a color family.
- Its value is light, medium, or dark.
- Its intensity can range from bright to dull.

The mixing up of the last two items—value and intensity—are where the majority of color mistakes occur. For example, brightness can overwhelm your pattern if what you really need is a light value.

We've included exercises in each chapter for block mock-ups to help you learn about value placement and combining color families. But how do you do a mock-up of a scrap block? Scrap quilts by their very nature make mock-ups useless, so we can't fall back to our position of making mock-ups to establish where the lights, darks, and medium fabrics will go to create our pattern.

The easiest way to organize scraps for a project is to sort the fabrics—regardless of color family—into piles of lights, mediums, and darks. Some scrap quilts, such as our old friend Log Cabin, need only light and dark values. Look over your pattern and see if you can identify where lights and darks have been used, and whether mediums are used at all. A black-and-white photocopy of the block or quilt will help discern value differences. Refer to "Value" on page 11 and "Intensity" for a review of those concepts.

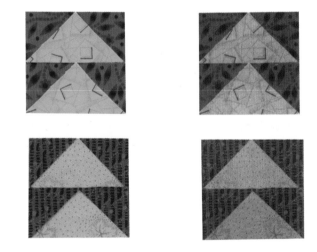

Make a few blocks from fabric and then check your choices by viewing them from a distance or using a reducing glass. This gives you a different look at your colors and fabrics. We get so close to our projects that all we see is the print on the fabric, the points that don't match, or the threads sticking out between the seams. All these things distract from the whole picture. We don't usually look at finished quilts from 15" away, so why do we make color decisions based on that distance?

NO LONELY PETUNIAS HERE

Remember, if there is only one of a bright or grayed fabric in a quilt, it will be lonely and shout, "Look at me!" Give it some company (something similar, but not necessarily the same), and then it will quiet down and have a conversation, making the whole quilt more interesting.

Two Plans for Scrap Quilts

To get you started on the path to successful scrap quilts, we've included two methods for you to try. The first begins with a multicolored print as your starting point. The second involves choosing color families.

Choose a Multicolored Print

Way back on page 9 we showed you a picture of some beautiful multicolored fabrics, and here is a good way to use them. They are a great jumping-off point for a scrap quilt if you remember the following tips. These tips can help you control your urge to include everything but the kitchen sink in the quilt.

- Use the colored dots on the selvage as a guide to selecting other fabrics, but don't be a slave to them—remember that each of those colors has a huge range of family members to choose from.

- Just because the colors appear on the selvage doesn't mean they have to be in equal proportions.

Choose a multicolored print that you love. If you can identify what it is that pleases you about the fabric, you are on your way to re-creating the same thing in your scrap quilt. Make a note of the colors used in your multicolored print, and then decide which color families they all belong to. Decide whether the colors in your print are bright (intense) or dull or somewhere in between. Maybe they are all clear but dark. They might all be very soft. Make a note of this. Then choose fabrics in these color families. Remember to choose as many as you can—lights, mediums, and darks. Again, this range of values will depend on whether your particular pattern needs that range of values.

Roughly estimate the proportions of the colors used in the print—this can help you analyze what you like about it. Remember that the proportions you use of each color family are up to you. Not crazy about blue? Or green? Use less of it than the others. It's *your* quilt, and it's fine to limit some color families.

Choose Color Families

If you need to give a more controlled look to your scrap quilt—and some of us do—simply choose color families you would like to work with and select all your fabrics within those color families.

Pick a color scheme or combination of colors using the color wheel—for instance, the split-complementary scheme using red-orange with blue and green—and start sorting fabrics into those color family groups. Then sort into the needed piles of light, medium, and dark, referring to "Value" on page 11 if you need a refresher course.

EXERCISE: Observe and Practice

Study multicolored fabrics and look closely at them to identify the colors and values used and the intensity of the colors. This will help you learn about using color more successfully. Make notes. Do the same with quilts that you admire. Remember that you can work with your color ideas on small projects such as baby quilts, wall hangings, or charity quilts before tackling your own bed-sized quilt.

We've included a "free-form" exercise here to help you practice discerning different values when using several or many colors.

Follow one of the plans for scrap quilts outlined at the beginning of this chapter.

Choose one of the smaller quilt projects in this book, such as "Chinese Coins," "Look Both Ways," or "City Mouse," to make as a scrap quilt. Because you will use many different fabrics, there are no specific amounts listed for cutting. Also, these are not large projects and you can still learn a lot, even if they present an "unexpected outcome." They can be passed along to a grandchild or charity.

When you make note of the colors you want to use, it's okay to call them names such as "teal" or "coral" or "buttercup," as long as you can find the color family on the color wheel they belong to. Identifying these colors this way will help you relate them to each other.

Check to see if there is a color combination (such as analogous, Next-Door Neighbors; or complementary, Family across the Road) that you'd like to try out. It's okay to choose some of your colors from a print and consider the rest of the colors accents. You don't need to represent them *all* again in your project.

Referring to your chosen pattern or project, make a note about what values were used where. For example, in "Chinese Coins," the block centers actually alternate light and dark across the quilt in rows. Slight differences in value and intensity make this interesting. Make some blocks using different colors and values.

Now for the fun part! This may be a new process to you, so persevere and be patient. Put blocks up on the design wall. The more you put up the better. Move them around, stand back, and look or use your reducing glass or binoculars. Take your time. Take a break from this and come back to it later. You have nothing to lose—any time spent practicing is valuable. Ionne says: Sometimes you can "sneak up" on your work or glance at it as you go by, and you may notice a fabric or block that needs to be in a different position. Refer back to "Color 101 Review" on page 20 if you need a refresher on value, intensity, and warm and cool colors. Any blocks that don't make it into the quilt can be pieced into the back; then your quilt back will be just as interesting as the front!

As a final step, refer to the color checklist on page 27. When you have an arrangement that pleases you, sew the blocks together and add your border. Quilt, bind, and enjoy the fact that you have accomplished something and learned something as well.

Now try this exercise using a project of your choice, but choose your own color combination!

Whenever you get stuck, take stock of your colors and decide if they can be grouped as warm or cool colors. Then choose an accent from the opposite group.

Sometimes less is more—you don't have to put every color into the quilt when you work with a multicolored print.

FAMILY GATHERING

We lived in the country when I was growing up in southern Ontario. Many times there were great get-togethers with lots of families and neighbors for weddings, dances, and anniversary parties. I was always amazed by the huge variety of colors flashing by as people danced and mingled. Children ran about in a riot of color. They were exciting, joyful times! These memories inspired this quilt—the white is for the brides' dresses and the dark is for the suits the grooms and their best men wore. Along with the white and dark, many colors danced across the polished floors in those country halls. What fun!

~Ionne

Materials

Yardage is based on 42"-wide fabric.

1⅓ yards of white tone-on-tone print for blocks and setting squares

1 yard *total* of assorted tone-on-tone and hand-dyed medium gray fabrics for blocks and setting squares

⅞ yard *total* of assorted dark tone-on-tone colors for blocks with white background

⅔ yard *total* of assorted medium tone-on-tone colors for blocks with medium gray background

½ yard of dark gray print 1 for blocks and setting squares

½ yard of dark gray print 2 for top and left side borders and binding*

½ yard of medium gray print for bottom and right side borders and binding*

¼ yard *total* of assorted light tone-on-tone colors for blocks with dark gray background

3 yards of fabric for backing

52" x 58" piece of batting

*If you prefer to cut your binding from one fabric, you'll need ½ yard for binding and ¼ yard each of the two different fabrics for the borders.

Cutting

From the white tone-on-tone print, cut:

6 strips, 3½" x 40"; crosscut into 66 squares, 3½" x 3½"

9 strips, 1½" x 40"; crosscut into 68 rectangles, 1½" x 5"

3 strips, 1¾" x 40"; crosscut into 68 rectangles, 1½" x 1¾"

Continued on page 81

Finished Quilt: 48" x 54" • Finished Block: 3" x 3"
Made by Ionne and Sharon

Continued from page 79

From the assorted dark colors, cut:

68 rectangles, 1½" x 5", and 68 rectangles, 1½" x 3¼", in matching pairs from the same fabric

From the assorted tone-on-tone and hand-dyed medium gray fabrics, cut a total of:

48 squares, 3½" x 3½"

48 rectangles, 1½" x 5"

48 rectangles, 1½" x 1¾"

From the assorted medium colors, cut:

48 rectangles, 1½" x 5", and 48 rectangles, 1½" x 3¼", in matching pairs from the same fabric

From dark gray print 1, cut:

2 strips, 3½" x 40"; crosscut into 13 squares, 3½" x 3½"

2 strips, 1½" x 40"; crosscut into 12 rectangles, 1½" x 5"

1 strip, 1½" x 40"; crosscut into 12 rectangles, 1½" x 1¾"

From the assorted light colors, cut:

12 rectangles, 1½" x 5", and 12 rectangles, 1½" x 3¼", in matching pairs from the same fabric

From medium gray print 2, cut:

3 strips, 2" x 40"

3 strips, 2½" x 40"*

From the dark gray print, cut:

3 strips, 2" x 40"

3 strips, 2½" x 40"*

*Cut 6 strips from one fabric if you are not using 2 fabrics to make a pieced binding.

Block Assembly

1. Sew a 1½" x 5" strip of white fabric to a 1½" x 5" dark colored strip; press the seam toward the darker fabric.

2. Sew a 1½" x 3¼" strip of the same colored fabric to the other side of the white strip. Press the seam toward the dark fabric.

3. Sew a 1½" x 1¾" rectangle of white fabric to the 5" colored strip; be sure to sew the longer side of the rectangle to the colored strip. Press toward the darker fabric.

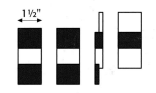

4. Crosscut the unit into three 1½"-wide segments as shown.

5. Sew the three segments together as shown, pressing toward the outside of the block.

6. Repeat steps 1–5 to make 68 blocks with white background fabric and dark-colored squares, 48 with medium gray background fabric and medium-colored squares, and 12 with dark gray background fabric and light-colored squares.

Quilt-Top Assembly

Refer to "Assembling the Quilt Top" on page 89 for tips on auditioning your blocks and sewing them together.

1. Referring to the quilt diagram, lay out the Nine Patch blocks and the setting squares in 17 rows.

2. Sew the blocks and squares together in rows, pressing the seams toward the setting squares.

3. Sew the rows together. Press the seams in one direction.

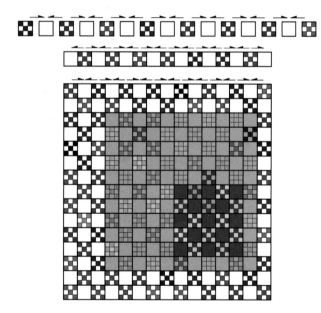

Adding the Borders

To balance the dark square in the lower-right corner of the quilt, we added a border in two values of gray—a medium and a dark. We placed the dark borders on the top and left sides of the quilt and the light gray on the bottom and right side. It's a subtle difference, but it adds interest and seems to counterbalance the darker areas of the quilt.

1. Sew the three 2" x 40" medium gray border strips together end to end. Measure the quilt through the center horizontally, cut a strip to that measurement, and sew it to the bottom of the quilt. Press the seam toward the border.

2. Measure the quilt through the center vertically. Cut the remaining medium gray strip to fit and sew it to the right side of the quilt. Press the seam toward the border.

3. Repeat steps 1 and 2 to add the 2"-wide dark gray border strips to the top and left side of the quilt. Press the seams toward the border.

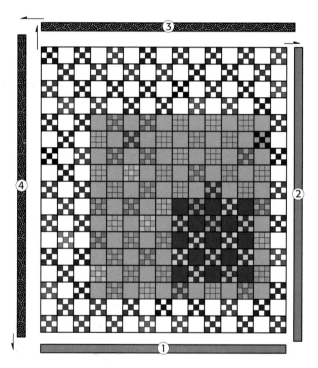

Finishing the Quilt

1. Referring to "Layering, Basting, and Quilting" on page 92, layer the batting, backing, and quilt top together. Baste with pins, or fuse if you're using fusible batting.

2. Quilt as desired.

3. For a binding made of one fabric, refer to "Binding" on page 94. For a binding that matches the borders of the quilt, see "Adding a Pieced Binding" on page 83.

ADDING A PIECED BINDING

To attach a binding that "matches" the borders of this quilt, you will need to sew on each side separately and butt the corners of your binding.

1. Sew the three binding strips of each color together using a diagonal seam to make one long strip. Cut the strips in half.

2. Cut two strips, 2½" x 4", off the end of one of the dark binding strips. Sew one to the end of each of the light binding strips using a straight seam. Press the seams open.

3. Press the four binding strips in half lengthwise with wrong sides together.

4. Sew the shorter dark binding strip to the top of the quilt using a ¼" seam. Pin a pieced lighter binding strip to the bottom of the quilt, aligning the seam of the darker gray piece with the border seam. Sew and then trim the ends of the binding even with the quilt. Press the binding strips away from the quilt.

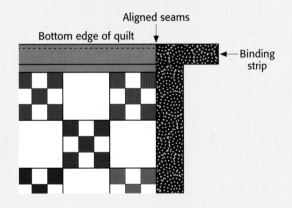

5. Sew the remaining dark binding strip to the left side of the quilt. Pin a lighter pieced binding strip to the opposite side of the quilt, aligning the seam with the border seam as before. Sew and press the binding away from the quilt. Trim the ends, leaving an extra ¼" beyond the ends of the top and bottom binding.

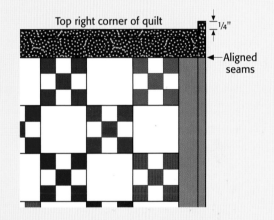

6. Fold the ¼" ends over, and then fold the binding strips to the back of the quilt, one side at a time, and hand sew them as for regular binding.

Since this book focuses on color, we don't have space to cover the basics of rotary cutting and piecing. If you need help with those techniques, look for one of the many good books available or take a class at a local independent quilt shop. In this section we include some helpful information specific to making the quilts in this book.

The Humble Nine Patch

Both of us love the unassuming little Nine Patch; it is a simple yet versatile block that is handy to have in your repertoire. It appears in many guises throughout this book, and we would like to share with you our favorite variations and how to piece them quickly and easily.

As you can tell from the quilt photos, we both love the scrappy look. We are also both lucky enough to have stashes that enable us to choose from 20 or 30 reds (or greens or blues or whatever). We'll show you how to make the basic Nine Patch with many different fabrics or with just a few, for those times when variety either isn't needed or isn't possible. We realize that building a stash takes time and if you're just getting started, the scrappy look isn't the easiest thing to accomplish.

(We've been told that when your stash gets beyond a certain point it can no longer be called a stash. You must then refer to it as a "stable"— STash Accumulated Beyond Life Expectancy. May we all be so lucky!)

By now you're familiar with the section about the importance of value, so the following instructions will make perfect sense to you. The basic Nine Patch block is made up of either five dark squares and four light ones, or the reverse; of course, each square can be a different fabric if you wish.

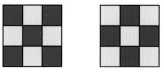

5 darks, 4 lights   5 lights, 4 darks

You can alter blocks by simply rearranging dark and light squares. For example, when making a Nine Patch for the outside row of blocks in "Jumping in the Leaves" (page 42), the lights were positioned in the middle of the block. For the corners we had them "turn the corner" as shown. This is a simple way to create a pieced border.

Similarly, to create diagonal lines as in "Look Both Ways" (page 51), the blocks were constructed with the dull orange squares crossing the block diagonally.

Making a Scrappy Nine Patch

The construction of a Nine Patch is simplicity itself when making a multiple-fabric block, which is just another name for a scrappy block. To make a finished 6" x 6" Nine Patch, follow these steps.

1. From assorted dark fabrics, cut five squares, 2½" x 2½", and place them on your design wall. From assorted light fabrics, cut four squares, 2½" x 2½", and place them between the dark squares.

2. Sew the squares together by chain piecing—instead of sewing two squares together and taking them out of the machine, you just feed the next two squares into the machine and continue sewing.

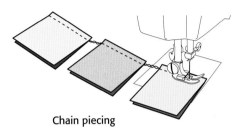

Chain piecing

3. Add a third square to each pair from step 2. Press the seams as desired (see "Pressing Matters" below right) and sew three units together to create the block.

THREAD SAVER

When you come to the end of your sewn patches you'll save a mile of thread and lots of time if you then sew over a piece of leftover fabric and cut the thread behind the foot to release your sewn pieces. When it's time to start sewing again, you don't have to search for the ends of the two threads and you never get "bobbin barf" when the tail of the bobbin thread gets sewn to the bottom fabric.

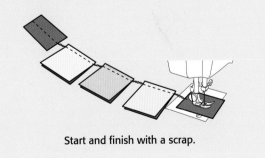

Start and finish with a scrap.

Strip-Pieced Nine Patches

To make many Nine Patches with the same fabrics, cut strips of the two colors or values, following size and color placement directions for your design.

1. Sew the strips together in groups of three as shown. Press seams toward the darker fabric.

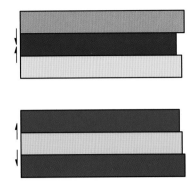

2. Trim and square up the ends.

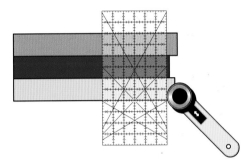

3. Crosscut the strips into segments in the size specified for your design.

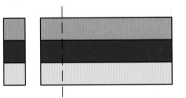

4. Sew together in groups of three and press the seams toward the rows with more dark fabrics.

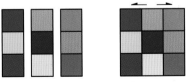

Pressing Matters

Pressing the seams in one direction isn't always the best solution, and it's OK to press them open when it suits you. It's almost impossible to have all seams pressed in opposite directions when sewing

Nine Patch blocks together side by side. During the making of "Jumping in the Leaves" (page 42), it made more sense to press the seams open so that when the blocks were joined there were not a lot of twisted seam allowances. Opposing seams will nest together for easy matching. For seams pressed open, pin just in front of the seam intersection, and they will line up just as nicely. Essentially, press seams to one side or open, whichever way you prefer. The Quilt Police will not be after you for any infractions.

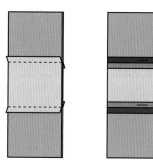

Opposing seams pressed toward darker fabric   **Seams pressed open**

PINNING TIP FOR PERFECT MATCHES

Ionne says: Placing a pin just before and just after an intersection is only the start of making those pesky intersections meet. Place the pin in the seam with a small "bite" right at the 1/4" seam allowance, right where the stitching line will be. Now, don't take the pins out until the needle of the sewing machine is almost at the pin. If you take the pin out before the presser foot is near the pin, the fabrics can still shift. Of course we never sew over pins. This can be dangerous; pins can shatter when the machine needle hits them, causing pieces to fly up into your face or down into the machine.

Half-Square Triangles

If you divide some of those squares in your basic Nine Patch into two triangles, replacing an unpieced square with a half-square triangle, just imagine how many more options you could have!

The Split Nine Patch in "Jumping in the Leaves" (page 42) or "Copper Beech" (page 67) was made of three half-square triangles and six plain squares.

Half-square triangle

Another variation is the Divided Nine Patch in "Rose Window" (page 48), which features only two half-square triangles. A third variation is the Friendship Star, with four half-square triangles. A variation of this block was used in "Twilight Zone" (page 39).

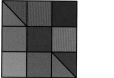

Divided Nine Patch   **Friendship Star**

There are many different ways to construct a square made up of two triangles, and they are all good methods. The method you choose depends on the desired result. A scrap Nine Patch will require that you make the squares individually. If you want to make many identical units, there are methods to make them quickly and efficiently.

Let's start with making each square individually—which is how you do it when you want lots of variety.

Making Scrap Half-Square Triangles

There is a formula that has been printed in thousands of books and articles about how big to cut the square that you will use to construct the half-square triangle. It has been proven mathematically and on the surface it is correct. But we are not machines, and we are not working with steel; we are working with fiber, which is flexible. So, instead of adding the usual ⅞" to the finished size of each square we add 1". (By "finished size" we mean after it's sewn into your quilt.) There are two advantages to this. One, it's a lot easier to find the 1" mark on your ruler, and two, when you have the square sewn together it is a tiny bit bigger than it has to be so you can trim it down. This guarantees a perfect square.

1. For a finished 2" square made up of two triangles, cut two squares, 3" x 3", from two different fabrics.

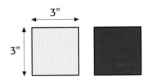

2. On the wrong side of the lighter of the two fabrics, draw a diagonal line from corner to corner.

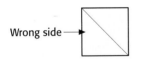

3. Place the two squares right sides together and sew ¼" from the drawn line on one side of the square, then turn the square around and sew ¼" from the line on the other side.

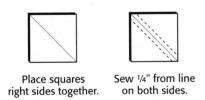

Place squares right sides together.   Sew ¼" from line on both sides.

4. Cut on the drawn line, open the resulting two units, and press the seams either open or in the direction you choose. Trim to a perfect 2½" square.

Cut on line.   Press seams.   Trim.

Mass Producing Half-Square Triangles

When you want to make lots of half-square triangles with the same two fabrics, there is a faster, easier way to do it called the grid method. The fabric needs to be big enough to draw a grid of four squares by three in the dimensions needed for your project. We recommend a grid measurement of 1" bigger than you want your finished half-square triangle to be. This gives you a bit of a margin around the outside edge that you can trim off to ensure a perfect size square every time.

Let's assume that you want to make 24 half-square triangles that are all the same and that finish at 2" x 2". You will need a grid of 12 squares that are 3" x 3". Your fabric will need to be at least 10" x 13".

1. Cut one 10" x 13" piece from each of the two fabrics. On the wrong side of the lighter of the two fabrics, draw the grid. Draw diagonal lines through the squares as shown in the diagram. You need one diagonal line running through each square. If you have diagonal lines crossing within a square, you've made a mistake.

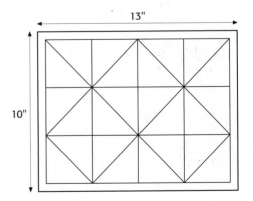

2. Place the two fabrics right sides together and sew ¼" from one side of the diagonal drawn

lines only. Then sew ¼" from the other side of the line.

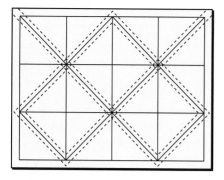

3. Cut on *every* drawn line. Press seams toward the dark fabric, or press seams open. Each square produces two half-square triangles. Trim each triangle square to the exact size.

Quarter-Square Triangles

Of course a quilter is never satisfied with just a few variations, so let's have a look at what you could do if you added a quarter-square triangle to the Nine Patch block. Our favorite is the Ohio Star block. It appears in "Midnight Stars" on page 71.

1. Cut two squares, each 1¼" bigger than you want your finished square to be.

2. Follow steps 2–4 of "Making Scrap Half-Square Triangles" on page 86, pressing the seams toward the darker of the two fabrics. Don't trim the pieced square.

3. Place the two pieced squares right sides together, alternating the position of the dark triangles. On the wrong side of one square, draw a diagonal line from corner to corner, crossing the seam of the half-square triangle.

4. Sew ¼" from both sides of the line, cut on the line, press the seams open, and trim.

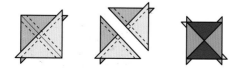

It's a simple thing to create quarter-square-triangle blocks using three or four colors.

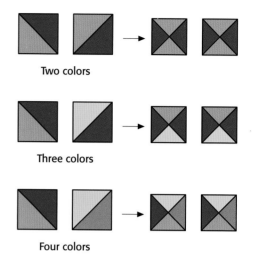

Two colors

Three colors

Four colors

The Snowball Block

Rather than cut an eight-sided "snowball"-shaped block and sew triangles to four corners, you can simply sew a small square to each corner of a larger square and then trim off the excess. This avoids working with tricky bias edges and ensures a perfect square when you're finished.

1. With right sides together, place a 2½" square onto the corner of a 6½" square. Draw a line from corner to corner on the small square.

2. Sew on the line. Trim the excess from the corner, leaving a ¼" seam allowance. Press toward the corner.

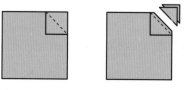

3. Repeat for all four corners to make the Snowball block.

NO-MARK SEWING ON THE DIAGONAL

To eliminate drawing a line from corner to corner on the smaller squares, you can make a guide on your sewing machine with a piece of masking tape. Put the needle in the down position, but leave the foot up. Place the tape so that the edge is right up against the needle and then, keeping it as straight as you can, pat it down. Remove any tape that is covering the feed dogs. Line up the corner of the small square with the needle, and line up the opposite corner with the edge of the masking tape. As you sew, keep the corner of your square lined up with the edge of the masking tape and your stitching will be on a perfect diagonal line.

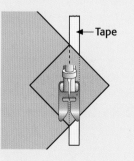

Assembling the Quilt Top

As you make your blocks, particularly when making a scrappy quilt, we recommend that you put them up on a design wall. A design wall is simply a vertical surface you can use to display your blocks while choosing the perfect spot for each one. One way of constructing a design wall is to cover foam core

with batting. The batting holds onto the blocks and the foam core allows you to pin if necessary. It's easy to manipulate the blocks to see the various settings possible with the blocks you've made. When you have your blocks in the absolute best setting, it's time to sew them together.

1. One easy way to get blocks from the design wall to the sewing machine is to take them off the wall by stacking them in rows. Keep the block from the top row on the top of each stack. Each stack represents a vertical row of the quilt.

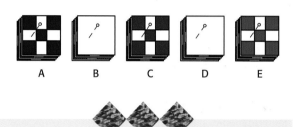

A   B   C   D   E

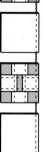

PIN POINTER

To keep from getting mixed up, insert a pin in the top block of each row so you always know which way is up.

2. Beginning with the top block from pile A and the top block from pile B, sew them together. Then you just take the next blocks in piles A and B and sew them together. This is a good time to chain piece.

3. When you have all the blocks from piles A and B sewn together, add all the blocks from pile C and so on.

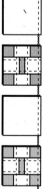

Chain piece piles A and B together.

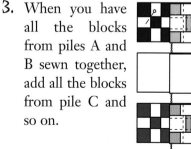

Add blocks from C.

4. When all the blocks are sewn together, press the seams in opposite directions from row to row. Here's an easy way to do it. With the chain-pieced rows wrong side up on your ironing board, press seams in each *alternate* row to the left. Turn the quilt top around and press the rest of the seams to the left. (Left-handers can press all seams to the right.) This ensures that all rows have seam allowances pressed in opposing directions.

5. Now it's time to sew the rows together. If you have been chain piecing, they are all in place and it's a simple matter of lining up seam lines and triangle points (if applicable) and sewing the rows together. Press the seams in one direction.

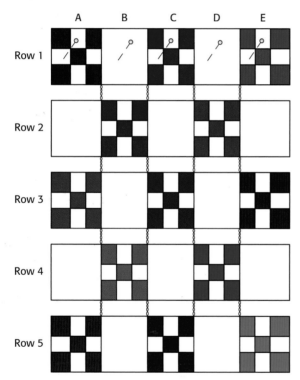

HOW QUILTING IS LIKE FISHING

We both do most of our designing using Electric Quilt 5. This software program offers a wonderful opportunity to try out different color schemes and settings without committing yourself to fabric. If you don't have a computer, you can still explore many possible settings for your blocks on a design wall before you sew them together. One word of advice—if you do find a beautiful setting for your blocks but want to try "just one more," be sure to take a picture of the one you have. There *is* such a thing as "the one that got away" in quilting!

Borders

The quilts in this book have three different types of borders: basic borders, borders with corner squares, and borders with mitered corners.

Basic Borders

1. Measure the length of your quilt through the center and mark the centers. Cut two strips to that measurement, piecing if necessary.

2. Center the border strip with the center of the quilt and sew with a ¼" seam. Press the seams toward the borders.

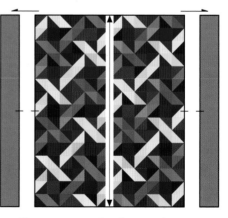

Measure center of quilt, top to bottom.
Mark centers.

3. Measure the width of your quilt through the center and mark the center. Cut two strips to that measurement, piecing if necessary.

4. Center the border strip with the center of the quilt and sew with a ¼" seam. Press the seams toward the borders.

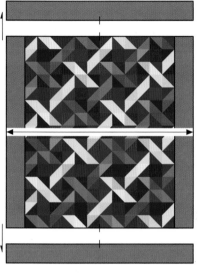

Measure center of quilt, side to side,
including border strips.
Mark centers.

Borders with Corner Squares

1. Measure the length and width of your quilt through the center, and mark the centers. Cut four border strips to these measurements, piecing if necessary.

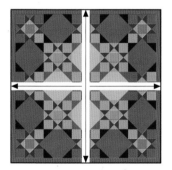

Measure center of quilt top
in both directions.

2. Centering the side border pieces with the sides of the quilt, sew with a ¼" seam. Press seams toward the border.

3. Cut corner squares to your measurement and sew one square to each end of the top and bottom border pieces. Press the seams away from the corner.

4. Centering the top and bottom border pieces with the quilt, making sure you line up the corner squares with the seams of the side border pieces. Sew with a ¼" seam. Press the seams toward the border.

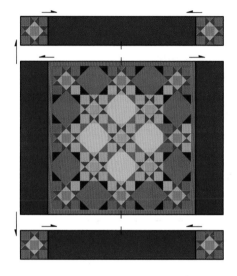

Borders with Mitered Corners

1. Measure the length and width of your quilt through the center.

2. Add twice the width of the borders plus 2" on each end (4" total, to be on the safe side) to the quilt dimensions from step 1. Cut the two side border strips and the two top and bottom border strips to those lengths.

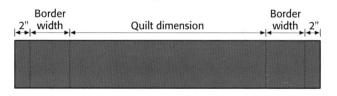

3. Find the center of one side border strip and pin it to the center of the side of the quilt.

4. Starting ¼" from the end, stitch to within ¼" of the other end. Backstitch at each end to secure the seam. Repeat for all four sides. Press the seams toward the border.

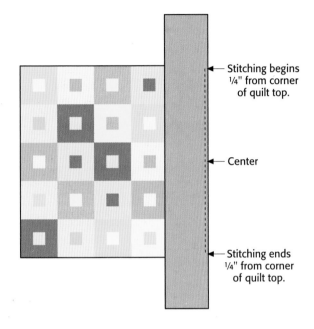

Stitching begins ¼" from corner of quilt top.

Center

Stitching ends ¼" from corner of quilt top.

5. To sew the mitered borders, first place the quilt on an ironing board. Layer the top border over the side border. Fold the top border piece at a 45° angle to the bottom piece and press. If you are using a stripe, put pins through the stripes, making sure they line up with the underneath stripe. I often use a basting stitch the first time I sew a mitered corner when using striped fabric. That way I can easily do it over again if it's not lined up properly. If I'm happy with the alignment, I adjust the stitch length and sew directly on the first stitching line, remembering to anchor my stitches at the beginning and end.

SECURE YOUR STITCHES

When you want to anchor your stitches starting exactly at a certain spot, put the needle into the fabric where you want to start. Then set your machine for a very short stitch length and sew for about ¼" to ⅜"—if you've ever had to rip out small stitches, you *know* how well-anchored this is!

6. Fold the two border pieces right sides together, and, if necessary, draw a pencil line on the crease so you can see where to sew.

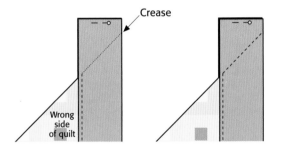

Crease

Wrong side of quilt

7. Stitch on the crease from the end of the previous stitching line to the outside edge. Repeat for all four corners.

8. Check on the right side to see that the miters are sewn correctly. Then trim the excess fabric, leaving a ¼" seam allowance. Press the seams open.

Layering, Basting, and Quilting

We each have our favorite method of layering and, as you might expect, they are different. Ionne prefers basting with safety pins, and Sharon is a fusible-batting aficionado. For a discussion of battings, see "Which Batting to Use?" on page 93.

When the quilt top is complete and marked as desired, you will assemble the quilt sandwich: the backing, batting, and quilt top. The backing and batting should be at least 4" larger than the quilt top. If your quilt is wider than your fabric width, you will need to piece the backing. Piece it either horizontally or vertically to make the most efficient use of your fabric.

1. Spread the backing, wrong side up, on a flat, clean surface. (If using a fusible batting, protect your tabletop with an old blanket.) Anchor the backing fabric with masking tape or clips. Be careful not to pull it too tight or stretch it out of shape.

2. Spread the batting over the backing, smoothing out any wrinkles.

3. Center the pressed quilt top, right side up, on top of the batting. Smooth out any wrinkles and make sure the edges of the quilt top are parallel to the edges of the backing.

4. To baste the layers together, use No. 2 rust-proof safety pins for machine quilting. Begin in the center and place pins in a grid about 6" to 8" apart. If you have chosen a fusible batting, fuse the layers together following the manufacturer's directions.

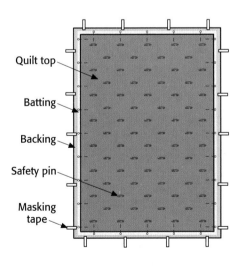

- Quilt top
- Batting
- Backing
- Safety pin
- Masking tape

5. For machine-guided quilting, use your walking foot. For free-motion quilting, drop the feed dogs and attach a darning foot to stitch the designs. Maurine Noble's *Machine Quilting Made Easy* (Martingale & Company, 1994) is a great resource if you'd like more information about machine quilting.

WHICH BATTING TO USE?

One thing we do agree upon is the brand of batting to use. We are both very fond of Hobbs Heirloom Cotton, which is 80% cotton and 20% polyester. It is also available as a fusible. The loft is enough to give interesting hills and valleys when quilted but not so thick that it is difficult to machine quilt. It requires quilting every 4½", but this isn't usually a problem as we both like to machine quilt. On those occasions when you want to do less quilting we recommend switching to Hobbs Organic with Scrim; this batting has a high percentage of cotton, but with the addition of a scrim you can leave up to 8" unquilted.

Hanging Sleeves

If you plan to add a hanging sleeve to the quilt, it's best to prepare the sleeve and pin it to the top of the quilt back so it can be sewn in with the binding.

1. Measure the width of your quilt and subtract 1". From the backing fabric, or another fabric similar to it, cut a piece 6" to 9" wide by that measurement and fold the ends under to make a hem. Stitch the hems.

6" to 9"

2. Before pinning the sleeve to the quilt top, press it lengthwise, wrong sides together, with one side extending ½" above the other. This will put a crease in the bottom of the sleeve that will be hand sewn to the back of the quilt. You want the sleeve to be relaxed enough to hold a hanging rod without making the front of the quilt bulge.

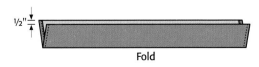

½"

Fold

3. Line up the raw edges with the raw edges of the top of the quilt, making sure the shorter portion is toward the back, and machine baste in place.

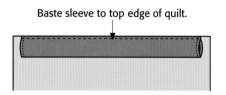

Baste sleeve to top edge of quilt.

4. The top of the sleeve will be machine sewn in with the binding, but the bottom must be hand stitched to the back of the quilt. When you do the hand stitching, push the top layer of the hanging sleeve up so that the crease you put in is visible along the bottom. Pin and blindstitch the sleeve to the back of the quilt along the crease. There will be plenty of space for the rod.

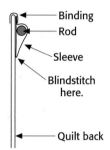

Binding
Rod
Sleeve
Blindstitch here.
Quilt back

Binding

We each have a preferred method for attaching bindings, so we've included both. You can choose whichever method you like.

Basic Binding from Ionne

My favorite binding is a double-fold binding using strips cut 2½" across the width of the fabric.

1. Trim the batting and backing even with the quilt top. Referring to "Hanging Sleeves" on page 93, add a hanging sleeve to the top edge of the quilt before adding the binding.

2. Cut enough strips to go around the perimeter of the quilt, adding 12" for joining strips and

mitering corners. Sew them together with a diagonal seam as shown. Press seams open.

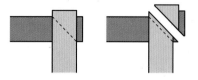

3. Fold the binding in half, wrong sides together, and press. Starting on a side of the quilt and leaving a 10" tail, use a ¼" seam allowance to stitch the binding to the quilt, keeping raw edges aligned. Stop stitching ¼" from the corner, and leave the needle down.

4. Raise the presser foot and turn the quilt a quarter turn counterclockwise.

5. Place a 2" square of scrap fabric behind the presser foot, lower the presser foot, and stitch *backwards* onto the far end of the scrap. (You want to leave room to manipulate the binding strip for the next edge.)

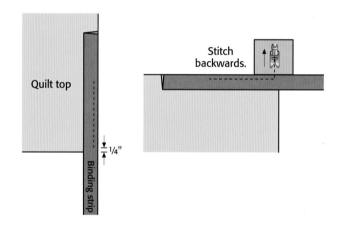

Quilt top

Stitch backwards.

¼"

Binding strip

6. Fold the binding away from the quilt, and then fold it back down onto itself so the fold is across the top edge of the quilt.

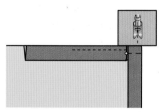

7. Stitch forward over the scrap and onto the quilt through all layers until you reach the next corner, stopping ¼" from the edge as before. Repeat the previous steps to the last corner.

8. Stop stitching 15" to 16" from where you started stitching. Remove the quilt from the machine and lay it on a flat surface. Open the folded strips and, keeping them flat against the quilt, fold one at a 45° angle to the quilt edge and the other in the opposite direction, so the folds just meet. Crease and mark the folds on the wrong side.

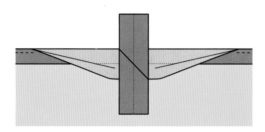

9. Pin so the creases match, using the marks on the wrong sides to align the creases, and stitch along the marked fold. Trim, press the seam open, refold the binding, and finish stitching the binding to the quilt.

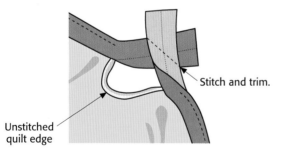

Stitch and trim.

Unstitched quilt edge

10. Turn to the back and slip-stitch the folded edge, mitering the corners as you come to them.

Bindings with "Waistband" Finish from Sharon

I learned this method of finishing the corners of bindings from a student in Greensboro, North Carolina, and I'm forever grateful for her help.

1. Measure the four sides of your quilt and add 1" to each. Cut four binding strips 2½" wide by that measurement.

2. If it's necessary to join the strips, sew them with a diagonal seam as shown on page 94. Trim and press seams open.

3. Fold the strips lengthwise, wrong sides together, and press.

4. Sew binding strips to two opposite sides of your quilt, trimming the ends flush with the ends of the quilt. Hand or machine sew the folded edge to the reverse side of the quilt.

Quilt top

Quilt back

5. Leaving a ½" tail at the beginning and end, sew a binding strip to the top and bottom of the quilt.

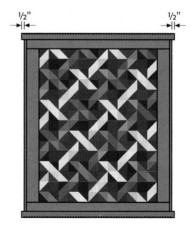

½"   ½"

6. With right sides together, sew the ends of the binding flush with the ends of the quilt. Make sure you keep the folded edge lined up with the folded edge of the seam allowance you have just sewn. Trim the seam allowance and turn right sides out.

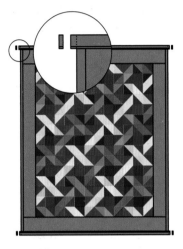

7. Hand or machine sew the folded edge to the reverse side of the quilt, as you did for the first two sides.

Labels

In 200 years some quilt historian is going to find your quilt in an antique store and will want to know who made it, where it was made, and when. So, imagine how happy he or she will be to turn your beautiful quilt over and see on the back:

For Mom, Catarina, with love from L. da Vinci Made in Florence, Italy July 1472

Now you know what Leonardo was doing between 1466 and 1472—it was his quilting period.

We're referring of course to a label, with all the necessary information—your name, where you live, and the date the quilt was made. Now, if you also added some relevant information about whom it was made for, or what inspired you, that little historian will just about burst with happiness.

Of course, the other reason for labeling your work is in case it gets lost on its way home from a show or display. We don't like to think that there are people in the world who would actually take a quilt that doesn't belong to them, but we know it happens, so putting your name on every quilt is very important.

We had lots of fun creating our labels because we were able to print out pictures of the book cover to work with.

COLOR FOR THE Terrified Quilter
PLAIN TALK, SIMPLE LESSONS, 11 PROJECTS

Family Gathering

48" x 54"
made by Ionne McCauley and
Sharon Pederson
February 2006

Made for our book –inspired by
the colourful clothing worn to
the country dances and
weddings of our childhood.